IMAGES
of Sport

WORCESTERSHIRE
COUNTY CRICKET CLUB

Don Kenyon, who captained Worcestershire to their first successes in 1964 and 1965, seen here batting at New Road where he scored 14,078 of his 37,002 first-class runs, including 31 of his 70 centuries.

IMAGES
of Sport

WORCESTERSHIRE
COUNTY CRICKET CLUB

Compiled by
Les Hatton

TEMPUS

First published 1999
Copyright © Les Hatton, 1999

Tempus Publishing Limited
The Mill, Brimscombe Port,
Stroud, Gloucestershire, GL5 2QG

ISBN 0 7524 1834 3

Typesetting and origination by
Tempus Publishing Limited
Printed in Great Britain by
Midway Clark Printing, Wiltshire

Some other cricket titles from Tempus Publishing:

Glamorgan CCC
Glamorgan CCC: The Second Selection
The Scarborough Festival
Somerset CCC
Yorkshire CCC

W.G. Grace leaves the field at New Road in 1899, having scored 175 for London County in a two-day non-first-class match. He appeared there again for London County in 1900, scoring 30 and 20 in his only first-class match at New Road.

Contents

Acknowledgements

The author would like to express his thanks to the following people for their assistance in the compilation of this book. Special thanks go to Bernard Bridgewater, Jean Kenyon and her daughter, Susan Jackson, Joan Grundy and Mike Vockins in the office at New Road and Peter Wynne-Thomas at Trent Bridge, Jill Smith and Betty and Ken Edwards. Many other people and organisations have been most helpful, including the Wolverhampton-based photographer Les Jacques, Mike Grundy, Annie Dendy at *Berrows Journal*, Tom Bader, Michael Dowty, Patrick Eagar, Ken Kelly, Ian Osbourne, Albert Wilkes, Airviews Manchester, *The Birmingham Post & Mail*, *The Daily Mirror*, S. & G. Press Agency, Keystone Press Agency, Universal Pictorial Press Agency and the ladies at Supa-Snaps in Bilston. I have tried, wherever possible, to consult and acknowledge possible owners of copyright. Any oversight is inadvertent, and the author will examine any further claims that might arise if called upon to do so.

Bibliography

Who's Who of Cricketers, Hamlyn 1993, Phillip Bailey, Phillip Thorn and Peter Wynne-Thomas; *The Wisden Book of Test Cricket 1877 to 1977*, Macdonald and Janes 1979, Bill Frindall; *John Wisden's Cricketers' Almanac* (various years); *Worcester CCC Yearbook* (1928-99); *Cricket Grounds of Worcestershire*, ACS 1985, Les Hatton; *Worcestershire CCC First-Class Records 1899-1996*, Limlow 1997, Les Hatton; *Wisden Book of Cricket Records*, Headline (third edition), Bill Frindall; *The History of Worcestershire CCC*, Christopher Helm 1989, David Lemmon; *Three Black Pears*, Worcestershire CCC 1998, Bernard Bridgewater; *Worcestershire CCC, A Pictorial History*, Severn House 1980, Michael Vockins; *The Cricket Statistician*, ACS Quarterly Journal (1973-79); *First-Class Cricket Matches 1892-1903*, ACS. Magazines include *Cricketer International* and *Wisden Monthly*.

Introduction

Worcestershire celebrated their centenary of first-class cricket at New Road in 1999 with a one-day match of 50 overs-a-side in coloured clothing on 7 May against the Australians and the result, because of rain, was decided on the Duckworth/Lewis method. Not quite the same as 4 May 1899 when Yorkshire were the visitors to New Road for the first ever first-class fixture to be played by the county. The *Berrows Journal* at the time reported: 'There was a bright genial sunshine for the opening day of this cricket match on the New Road Ground. Everything was of the happiest augury for the debut of Worcestershire in first-class cricket. Mr Foley, Mr Isaac, and others had been at work from soon after dawn to put the finishing touches to the arrangements. Everything looked as pleasant as one would desire'. Yorkshire won the toss and batted and were immediately in trouble when George Wilson bowled J.T. Brown, of Driffield, with the third ball of the first over and continued his remarkable debut with another seven wickets, finishing with 8-70. These are the second best figures for a County Championship debut, bettered only by S.J. Whitehead for Warwickshire at Trent Bridge in 1894. Yorkshire won a low scoring game by 11 runs and the *Sportsman* of the day said: 'Though beaten, the Worcestershire eleven gave many evidences of sterling merit, and nothing finer than their all-round work in the field could be desired'.

By the end of the season Worcestershire had beaten Leicestershire and Derbyshire at New Road, drawn five, lost five and finished twelfth out of fifteen in the table. For the first few years Worcestershire were given the nickname 'Fostershire' because of the seven brothers from Malvern who, between them, made 608 first-class appearances from 1899 until 1934. On two occasions in 1905, against the Australians at Worcester and Somerset at Taunton, four of them played together. Harry was the first captain, R.E. ('Tip') a Test cricketer (and Worcestershire's first *Wisden* Cricketer of the Year in 1901) and their sister married South African born William Greenstock, who made four appearances for the county, with their son, John, making his debut in 1924 and going on to play thirteen times.

Worcestershire's best season before the Second World War was to finish as joint runners-up, with Yorkshire, to Nottinghamshire in 1907, but they were usually found in the lower reaches of the Championship table. They were at the foot of the table for three successive seasons from 1926 and went 53 matches without a first-class win between 1927 and 1929. In 1920 they had misfortune to lose twelve of their eighteen Championship matches by an innings, nine of these being during a ten-match sequence. During this period in the twenties Worcestershire were hard up and many of their cricketers were amateurs – and some of them not very good ones at that. In the 1922 and 1923 seasons as many as thirty-seven different players were used in the Championship, twenty-eight of them amateurs in 1922 and twenty-three of them in 1923.

During this period and into the early thirties, Fred Root was the bowler who did most of the work and at the end of his Worcestershire twelve-season career he had taken 1,387 wickets, including 207 in 1925 – the only season in which a Worcestershire bowler has taken 200 wickets. This was a remarkable career when one considers that with all the innings defeats during this time he usually only bowled in the opponent's first innings! The thirties heralded a slight improvement with Cyril Walters at the helm and the emergence of Reg Perks, Peter Jackson, Dick Howorth and 'Doc' Gibbons led to a seventh place final position in the 1939 Championship table – their best since 1908. This was a promising side, led by Charles Lyttelton, including Perks, Jackson, Howorth and Gibbons, to be joined by Eddie Cooper, Charlie Palmer, 'Roly' Jenkins, Sid Martin and Syd Buller. Unfortunately, with six blank seasons because of the Second World War, the side, as with many others, was almost broken up in 1946.

My Worcestershire cricket watching began in 1946, mostly at the venues near my home – Dudley, Stourbridge and Kidderminster – with a visit to New Road being quite rare in the forties and early fifties (although my father did get me there for Bradman's 1948 Australians). A new name had arrived at Worcester around this time, a name that was going to change all those bad days. The name was, of course, Don Kenyon, who has still scored more first-class runs for Worcestershire than any other batsman. He made his debut in 1946 and when he retired at the end of the 1967 season he had scored 34,490 runs (including 70 hundreds) and led the county to an incredible dream. The County Championship was won for the first time in 1964 and again in fine style the following season, when they won ten of their last eleven matches (drawing the other one). The stalwarts of this side were Martin Horton, Ron Headley, Tom Graveney, Roy Booth, Duncan Fearnley, Norman Gifford, Len Coldwell, Jack Flavell and Doug Slade, with great back-up from Bob Carter, Brian Brain and Jim Standen, who were joined by Basil D'Oliveira and Alan Ormrod for 1965. One-day cricket had arrived for the first-class counties and Worcestershire appeared in the first Gillette Cup final at Lord's in 1963, losing to Sussex (then led by Ted Dexter) by 14 runs – although Norman Gifford did get the Man of the Match award. Don led them to another final in 1966, but this time they were beaten by neighbours Warwickshire.

Glenn Turner joined Worcestershire in 1967 and was followed by Vanburn Holder in 1968. These two were model overseas cricketers during their time at New Road. Turner made his debut against the 1967 Pakistanis and opened with Don for a short-lived 14-run partnership. When he left for his New Zealand home at the end of the 1982 season he had scored 22,298 runs with a new Worcestershire record of 72 centuries. A wrist injury in the Second Test against India caused the new captain to miss the latter part of the 1971 season. Norman Gifford had taken over from Tom Graveney, but the county were to use four different captains because of this injury and Test Match calls. Ron Headley, one of the four, steered Worcestershire to their first one-day trophy when they won the John Player Sunday League on superior run-rate from runners-up Essex. The Championship was won again in 1974, snatched from Hampshire and wonderfully orchestrated by Norman Gifford: Worcestershire went into the last match of the season at Chelmsford two points behind leaders Hampshire, who were due to play Yorkshire at Bournemouth. Rain delayed the start and Gifford, having won the toss, asked Essex to bat. The home side reached 42 without loss before the captain came on and caused havoc and ten wickets fell for 42 runs, Gifford taking 7-15. The game at Bournemouth was abandoned without a ball being bowled so the four bowling points gave Worcestershire their third Championship title.

The next major era in Worcestershire's history was under the leadership of Phillip Neale, who took over the captaincy from Glenn Turner for the 1982 season. The nucleus of another good side was developing with the Second XI Championship won in 1982 and the arrival of the likes of Tim Curtis, Richard Illingworth and Phil Newport. A young man from Zimbabwe, Graeme Hick, made people sit up when he made his debut at the end of the 1984 season, scoring 82 not out at The Oval – the rest is history. The final pieces of the jigsaw were coming together when Neal Radford and Steve Rhodes moved south in 1985 and Ian Botham and Graham Dilley moved north in 1987. Silverware was won thick and fast with the Sunday League title in 1987 and 1988, the County Championship in 1988 and 1989 and, after six unhappy visits to Lord's, Worcestershire beat Lancashire to take the Benson and Hedges Cup in 1991. Tim Curtis took over the captaincy in 1992 and led Worcestershire to the runners-up spot in the County Championship the following season. There was success again at Lord's when they beat Warwickshire in the 1994 NatWest Trophy final, although Curtis resigned during the 1995 season and Tom Moody has held the post since.

Many people have enjoyed Worcestershire's 100 years of first-class cricket. The highlight for me has to be the 1964 County Championship success – a dream that was unthinkable when may father was a young man but wonderfully enjoyable when it happened.

Les Hatton
September 1999

One

Fostershire

Paul Foley was the
inspiration in raising
Worcestershire to first-class
status. He made only one
first-class appearance, for
MCC, scoring 8 and 13
against Somerset at Taunton
in 1891, but appeared for
Worcestershire in their non
first-class days between 1880
and 1896 and was secretary
and treasurer of the club from
1892 until 1909. Foley, more
than anyone, was responsible
for the formation of the
Minor Counties
Championship in 1895 and
was the first secretary of that
competition.

Worcestershire *v.* Surrey Second XI at The Oval in 1893. From left to right, back row: A. Millward, R.D. Burrows (twelfth man), S. Raynor, T. Rollins, Page (scorer), W. Greenstock, A. Smith. Middle row: Edwards (wicketkeeper), C. Toppin (captain), P.H. Foley, E.P. Jobson, H.K. Foster. Front row: P.H. Latham, W.L. Foster, F.G. Willoughby. The two eldest of the Foster brothers, H.K. (aged nineteen) and W.L. (who was eighteen and still at Malvern College), are pictured with Percy Latham, a former Malvern College schoolboy who went to Cambridge University and gained Blues in 1892, 1893 and 1894, captaining the side in 1894. He went on to play 40 matches for Sussex between 1898 and 1906, scoring 93 on his Championship debut against Lancashire.

Worcestershire *v.* Berkshire, 1897. From left to right, back row: J. Edge (umpire), A. Millward, F.L. Bowley (twelfth man), G.F. Wheldon, R.D. Burrows, R.E. Foster. Middle row: E.P. Jobson, E.G. Bromley-Martin, H.K. Foster, P.H. Foley, G.E. Bromley-Martin. Front row: T. Straw, E.G. Arnold (often caught on camera with a cigarette in his mouth), A. Bird. This was the first county match at New Road and visitors Berkshire were beaten by an innings and 24 runs. Worcestershire had great success in the Minor Counties competition, sharing the championship with Durham and Norfolk in 1895 and winning it outright in 1896, 1897 and 1898.

Worcestershire v. Yorkshire 4-6 May 1899. *Above:*
The team that played in the match consisted of,
from left to right, back row: G.F. Wheldon, G.A.
Wilson, Mr P.H. Foley (secretary), E.G. Arnold,
R.D. Burrows. Middle row: W.L. Foster, E.G.
Bromley-Martin, H.K. Foster (captain), R.E. Foster,
G.E. Bromley-Martin. Front row: T. Straw
(wicketkeeper), A. Bird. Three of the seven Foster
brothers appeared for Worcestershire in this
opening match at New Road, with W.L. making
his first-class debut along with Arnold, Bird, E.G.
Bromley-Martin, Burrows, Straw and Wheldon.
There were several combinations of the brothers
appearing together, but on only two occasions did
four of them play together. In 1905, H.K., R.E.,
W.L. and G.N. were in the same sides against the
Australians at New Road and against Somerset at
Taunton. *Right:* The scorecard from the match.
Worcestershire finished their inaugural season in
the County Championship in twelfth place with
two wins, both at New Road, against Leicestershire
(by 122 runs) and Derbyshire (by an innings and
218 runs). In the latter match H.K. hit 162, G.E.
Bromley-Martin 129 and W.W. Lowe 102 not out
in a total of 557. W.L. topped the club's batting
averages, scoring 954 runs at 41.48, and George
Wilson took most wickets with 86 at 21.53.

WORCESTERSHIRE
v.
YORKSHIRE.
MAY 4, 5 and 6, 1899.

YORKSHIRE.

		1st			2nd
Brown b Wilson		0	c Straw b Burrows		29
Tunnicliffe b Wilson		16	c Wheldon b Arnold		7
Denton b Wilson		19	c Straw b Wilson		0
F. Mitchell b Wilson		32	run out		22
Moorhouse b Wilson		2	b Burrows		8
Wainwright c H. Foster b Wilson		35	c Arnold b E. B. Martin		86
Hirst c R. Foster b Wilson		14	c Wilson b E. Bromley Martin		35
Haigh b Wilson		1	c R. E. Foster b E. B. Martin		4
Rhodes b Arnold		4	c W. Foster b Wilson		1
Hunter not out		1	not out		7
Brown (Darfield) c and b Arnold		9	c Wheldon b E. B. Martin		2
Extras		6	Extras		4
Total		139	Total		205

WORCESTERSHIRE.

1st INNINGS.		2nd INNINGS.	
H. K. Foster c Brown b Rhodes	38	b Rhodes	0
G. Bromley Martin b Haigh	0	c Tunnicliffe b Rhodes	12
Arnold b Haigh	43	c Tunnicliffe b Hirst	33
R E. Foster run out	15	b Brown	32
W. L. Foster run out	0	b Haigh	22
Wheldon not out	47	b Brown	4
E. Bromley-Martin b Haigh	0	c Sub. b Brown	8
Bird c Wainwright b Rhodes	14	c Mitchell b Brown	0
Burrows b Hirst	13	b Brown	0
Wilson c Mitchell b Hirst	9	b Brown	2
Straw b Wainwright	9	not out	0
Extras	21	Extras	9
Total	211	Total	122

Umpires—Messrs. Farlow and Richards.

NEXT THURSDAY and FRIDAY—WORCESTERSHIRE v. NOTTS.

During the match against Hampshire at New Road in July 1905, W.L and R.E. Foster became the first brothers to each score two separate hundreds in the same match. In the first innings they shared a partnership of 161 in 90 minutes and in the second they added 219, both stands being for the third wicket. W.L. scored 140 in 180 minutes (with 16 fours) in the first innings and 172 not out (21 fours) in the second and R.E. 134 in 165 minutes (15 fours) and 101 not out (11 fours). This achievement remained a brotherly record until the Chappells, Ian and Greg, both scored centuries in each innings at Basin Reserve, Wellington for Australia against New Zealand in March 1974. The Foster brothers are seen leaving the field after this epic performance, to be met by older brother and captain, H.K. This was the only season that W.L. played cricket for Worcestershire regularly and this in itself was only made possible because he was invalided home from army service in the Middle East. He made frequent visits home, with odd appearances here and there either as Captain Foster or Major Foster. During his army career, which began at Woolwich Academy in 1892, he was awarded the DSO for gallantry in Somalia. On leaving the army he was made CBE in recognition of his work for the Gunners' prisoner of war fund during the First World War. R.E. was at Oxford University at the time that Worcestershire became a first-class county and captained the university side in 1900. He went on to take the captaincy of Worcestershire for one season in 1901. He went on the MCC tour to Australia in 1903/04, making an historic Test Match debut with an innings of 287 at Sydney – which is still the highest score on a Test debut and remained the highest score in Test cricket until Andy Sandham hit 325 against the West Indies in 1930. Between that debut and 1907 he played in eight Tests, captaining England in three of them against South Africa in 1907. R.E. was a fine all-round sportsman, winning blues also at soccer, golf and rackets, but suffered poor health and died in 1914 at the early age of thirty-six. At The Oval, where Worcestershire were the visitors, the luncheon interval was extended as a mark of respect as his funeral was taking place at that time

R.E. (left) and W.L. pictured together after their historic achievement against Hampshire.

H.K. (Harry) Foster captained Worcestershire for twelve seasons, initially in 1899 and 1900, then his brother R.E. (Tip) took over for 1901, before Harry resumed from 1902 until 1910 and then again in 1913. Harry played for Worcestershire more times than his other six brothers and when he retired after the 1925 season he had scored 15,053 runs for the county at 35.33 with 28 centuries. Two of them were turned into doubles, the first of these, in 1903, was 216 in two-and-three-quarter hours at New Road against Somerset – 250 runs being put on with Fred Bowley, who made 148, for the second wicket. The Worcestershire total of 590, which also included 112 by Fred Wheldon, was their best so far and it led to an innings and 109 runs win, with Wilson taking 6-76 in the Somerset first innings and Albert Bird 5-97 in the second. New Road was also the scene for his other double century in 1908, when he scored 215 against Warwickshire in three hours and forty minutes with a five and thirty fours – adding 221 for the third wicket with John Cuffe in two hours. Harry made his first-class debut in 1894 with Oxford University against Mr A.J. Webbe's Team, scoring 11 and 59 in a side that was captained by the legendary C.B. Fry and he gained his 'Blue' that season and in the following two. An all-round sportsman, he won a 'Blue' at racquets and went on to take the English Amateur Racquets Championship singles title at the Queen's Club on six consecutive occasions. He also won the doubles eight times, partnering brothers W.L. and B.S. in some of them. The only cricket representative honours he received were ten appearances for the Gentlemen against the Players, for whom he made his debut in 1896 under the leadership of W.G. Grace at The Oval, scoring 72 and sharing a sixth-wicket partnership of 107 with Surrey's Walter Read. At the end of the 1914 season, after playing just one match, he was presented with a testimonial amounting to £300 for his services to Worcestershire cricket – who was to know that he would return briefly after the First World War? He was the first Worcestershire cricketer to become an English Test selector, serving in 1907, 1912 and 1921 and, after leaving the game, he became an estate agent in Hereford and was awarded the MBE for services to agriculture during the First World War. His son, Christopher, played three matches for Worcestershire in 1927, scoring 34 runs in five innings with a best of 11 not out against The New Zealanders at New Road. Harry died in Hereford on 23 June 1950 in his seventy-seventh year.

George Wilson made a stunning first-class debut for Worcestershire in that much mentioned first match against Yorkshire in 1899, taking 8-70 in the first innings and 2-69 in the second – an effort that deserved much more than a defeat by 11 runs. The only batsman that escaped him in both innings was J.T. Brown, their number eleven from Darfield, and he had David Denton twice. He was the first Worcestershire bowler to take 100 wickets in a season when he finished with 119 at 22.92 in 1900 and the first to do the hat-trick when he had W.G. Quaife leg-before, then bowled F.G. Robinson and L.C. Braund with successive balls at New Road against W.G. Grace's London County in the same season. In 1901 he had a purple patch of five 5-wicket performances, beginning at Lord's with 5-71 and 5-58 against the MCC, 5-30 and 5-66 at Bath against Somerset and 6-61 at Maidstone against Kent. His career came to an end in 1906 after 154 matches with 719 wickets at 23.82 and a career best batting of 78 against London County (just before taking that first hat-trick).

William Burns was born in Rugeley, Staffordshire. He joined Worcestershire in 1903 as an amateur and left at the end of 1913 to settle in Canada. He was a fine all-rounder who bowled fast, but the validity of his action was often in question. At Worcester during his last season he scored 102 not out against Gloucestershire in less than two hours with a five and 12 fours in a total of 529-4 declared, a total boosted by Bowley (210) and Pearson (106). When the visitors replied Burns performed the hat-trick by having A.E. Dipper caught behind by Ernie Bale, J.W.W. Nason caught by Bowley and then bowling C.S. Barnett. At the time only W.G. Grace (1874) and the Australian George Giffen (1884) had scored a century and completed the hat-trick in the same first-class match. In 1909 at Edgbaston against Warwickshire he recorded his career best batting of 196 including 17 fours (see page 21). Burns returned to England at the outbreak of the First World War and enlisted with the Worcestershire Regiment but was killed in action at Contalmaison in France on 7 July 1916.

WORCESTERSHIRE COUNTY CRICKET CLUB.

OFFICIAL SCORE CARD. PRICE 1D.

WORCESTERSHIRE v. SOUTH AFRICANS

JULY 15th, 16th and 17th 1901.

SOUTH AFRICANS.

1st INNINGS.		2nd INNINGS.	
1 W. Shalders st Gaukrodger b S. Hayward	51	lbw b Pearson	32
2 L. J. Tancred b Wilson G.	12	b Bannister	34
3 A. Reide b Pearson	34	c Gaukrodger b Wilson G.	22
4 M. Hathorn b Simpson-Hayward	90	lbw b Pearson	0
5 J. H. Sinclair c S. Hayward b Pearson	3	c R. E. Foster b Bannister	14
6 M. Bisset b Wilson, G.	6	b Wilson, G.	0
7 A. V. C. Bisset b Wilson, G.	0	b Wilson, G.	23
8 C. F. Prince b Wilson, G.	35	b Wilson, G.	7
9 R. Graham not out	23	c Fereday b Bannister	0
10 J. J. Kotze b Bannister	29	b Wilson, G.	0
11 G. A. Rowe b Wilson, G.	0	not out	0
Extras	9	Extras	8
Total	293	Total	140

Wickets . 1 2 3 4 5 6 7 8 9 10
Runs ... 44 69 134 138 154 160 226 242 292 293 } 433
2nd innings 69 75 76 99 106 119 138 139 140 140 }

WORCESTERSHIRE.

1 Bowley c A. Bisset b Rowe	12	c M. Bisset b Graham	36
2 Pearson c Shalders b Kotze	10	c and b Graham	1
3 A. W. Isaac c Tancred b Kotze	16	c and b Rowe	42
4 R. E. Foster c Prince b Kotze	25	b Graham	0
5 Wheldon c Graham b Kotze	0	c M. Bisset b Graham	7
6 G. Simpson-Hayward c Graham b Sinclair	21	b Kotze	52
7 Fereday c M. Bisset b Sinclair	37	c M. Bisset b Graham	5
8 Gaukrodger not out	32	c Sinclair b Graham	24
9 Wilson (G.) c Prince b Sinclair	8	c Sinclair b Graham	4
10 Wilson (H.) c Graham b Kotze	8	st M. Bisset b Graham	5
11 Bannister c Sinclair b Graham	44	not out	15
Extras	10	Extras	18
Total	224	Total	209

Wickets... 1 2 3 4 5 6 7 8 9 10
Runs ... 27 45 66 81 82 121 142 152 212 224 } 433
2nd innings... 11 27 39 42 56 127 173 178 201 209 }

Umpires—Messrs. V. Titchmarsh and G. Bean.

(vertical text left margin: JULY 18, 19, 20—WORCESTERSHIRE v. SURREY.*)*

(vertical text right margin: JULY 18, 19, 20—WORCESTERSHIRE v. SURREY.*)*

The South Africans were the first tourists to visit New Road and, under the leadership of Murray Bisset, they arrived there in July 1901. On the tour so far they had won two and lost seven of their matches against first-class counties. The visitors won the toss and batted. At the close of play on the second day Worcestershire were 84-5 with Arthur Isaac 20 not out and George Simpson-Hayward 12 not out. They continued their partnership until Isaac was bowled by George Rowe for 42 with the score at 127. Robert Graham was on the way to a career best 8-90 when the last man, Harry Wilson, came to the wicket with 9 required for victory. Eight runs, five of them to Wilson, were hit before Bissex stumped Wilson off Graham for the game to end in a tie – Worcestershire's first. The county recorded their first County Championship tie in 1939 at Kidderminster when Somerset needed 6 to win with the last pair – Sam Weaver, the former Chelsea and Newcastle United long-throw specialist, and Horace Hazell – together. With the fourth ball of the last over Dick Howorth bowled Hazell with the scores level. Worcestershire's third, and latest, tie took place at Trent Bridge in 1993 when a throw from the square-leg boundary by Adam Seymour just beat Andy Pick, going for the second (match-winning) run, off the last ball.

Worcestershire had the audacity to challenge for the County Championship in 1907, finishing as joint runners-up with mighty Yorkshire to Nottinghamshire. The team is, from left to right, back row: J.A. Cuffe, F.A. Pearson, R.D. Burrows, F.L. Bowley, G.W. Gaukrodger. Middle row: R.E. Foster, G.H.T. Simpson-Hayward, H.K. Foster, W.B. Burns, G.N. Foster. Front row: E.G. Arnold (once more with a cigarette in his mouth), A. Bird. Worcestershire were led from the front by Harry Foster, who scored 1,085 Championship runs at 41.73 and he was assisted by his brother Tip with 753 at 41.83. The professionals provided excellent support with 'Dick' Pearson scoring 906 and Fred Bowley 784. Australian import John Cuffe took the bowling honours with 100 Championship wickets. 'Tip' Foster captained England in the three Test Matches against South Africa during that Summer and Arnold played in the first two of them.

Tom Straw kept wicket for Worcestershire from 1899 until the end of the successful 1907 season. He was a lower order batsman, scoring 600 runs at 10.71 besides holding 122 catches and taking 12 stumpings. He was born in Hucknall Torkard in Nottinghamshire on 1 September 1870 and first played for Worcestershire in 1894, before first-class status had been achieved, and signed an agreement with Paul Foley for £3 a week for that first season. The record books show that he is the only batsman to have been dismissed twice for obstructing the field and both occurred against local rivals Warwickshire. The first was in August 1899 at New Road when Warwickshire won easily by 204 runs and was followed by the same misdeed, this time at Edgbaston in 1901, when the home team won another one-sided match by an innings and 22 runs.

There was a mystery for a long time over the birthplace of wicketkeeper George Gaukrodger. Early Association of Cricket Statisticians publications gave it as Belfast, but Yorkshire statistician Darren Senior researched the Gaukrodger family and Leeds on 11 September 1877, was the final result. George joined Worcestershire in 1900, served a two year qualification period, and made his Championship debut in 1903 at Hove, replacing Straw. At Tunbridge Wells in 1907 he took four first-innings catches and stumped Frank Woolley and Edward Humphreys off Simpson-Hayward's underarm lobs. Six dismissals is still a Worcestershire best in the Championship but he now shares the record with Hugo Yarnold (1949), Rodney Cass (1973), Gordon Wilcock (1974) and Steve Rhodes (1988 and 1989). Gaukrodger had scored 2,230 career runs by the time he left for the Bradford League with a best of 91 at Liverpool in 1903 (adding 167 for the fifth wicket with H.K. Foster). His 229 dismissals, including 60 stumpings, puts him in seventh position in the list of most dismissals in a Worcestershire career.

George Simpson-Hayward, another of the long line of former Malvern schoolboys, missed the opening match against Yorkshire in 1899 and, like Straw, made his Championship debut at Hove in the next match. During his career he was probably the best known under-arm bowler in the game and bowled them for England in South Africa in five Test Matches in 1909/10, taking 23 wickets in the series. He captained Worcestershire in 1911 and 1912 and, during the first of these seasons, scored his career best 130 against Oxford University. The First World War ended his cricket career when he had taken 362 wickets for Worcestershire, including 24 five-wickets in an innings performances. At Lord's in 1909 he inspired the county to their first win at Headquarters with 10-107 in the match. In the second innings of this game he had career best figures of 7-54 when Middlesex were dismissed for 235 leaving Worcestershire needing 31 runs to win which they duly achieved, for the loss of three wickets.

When John Cuffe made his debut for Worcestershire against Oxford University in 1903 he became the first of a long line of overseas professionals to appear for the club. However, he had to serve a qualifying period and played in just six non-Championship matches before 1905. Arriving from Australia, having played just one match for New South Wales in 1902/03, he played an important role in the side that finished joint runners-up to champions Nottinghamshire in 1907 with 100 championship wickets and 509 runs. During that season he shared a ninth wicket partnership of 181 with Dick Burrows against Gloucestershire at New Road (which is still Worcestershire's best for that wicket). The best of his four Worcestershire hundreds was 145 at Bournemouth in 1905 where he added 122 for the third wicket with W.E.C. Hutchings and 113 for the fourth with Ted Arnold before he was run out. Bournemouth was a happy hunting ground for Cuffe as he performed the hat-trick there in 1911 when he dismissed H.W.M. Yates, E.M. Sprot and H.C. McDonnell with successive balls. Cuffe's career ended like many others with the start of the First World War and he moved into League cricket, coached at Wrekin College and, in 1931, joined Repton College as coach. Tragically, he ended his life in May of that year by jumping from a bridge in Burton into the River Trent.

Fred Bowley was the first Welsh-born Worcestershire cricketer, having come into this world in the shadow of the Brecon Mountains in 1873. He missed the first match in 1899 but appeared at Hove against Sussex in the second, ending the season with only 67 runs from nine visits to the crease – not the kind of beginning you would expect from the man who was to become the first Worcestershire batsman to aggregate 20,000 runs and who was, until beaten by Glenn Turner in 1982, the holder of the highest innings score (276 at Dudley against Hampshire in 1914). On that occasion Bowley batted for almost five hours, hitting 2 sixes, a five and 33 fours and reached his century before lunch on the first day – the fifth time he had achieved this in his career. He completed this feat for the sixth time in 1920 at Leyton when he was 125 not out at lunch against Essex and only Jack Hobbs (13) and W.G. Grace (7) have scored more hundreds before lunch on the first day than Bowley. He ended his career after one match in 1923 with 20,750 runs at 29.72 and 38 hundreds and joined Glamorgan on a three year contract as coach at £400 per annum.

Worcestershire CCC, under the trees at New Road, 1908. From left to right, standing: Mr Barrs (dressing room attendant), E.G. Arnold, J.A. Cuffe, F.L. Bowley, R.D. Burrows. Seated: G.N. Foster, G.H.T. Simpson-Hayward, H.K. Foster (captain), W.B. Burns, W.L. Foster, F.A. Pearson, F. Hunt, A. Bird.

Albert Bird was a professional cricketer with a strong family sporting background, having a brother, William, who played for both Warwickshire and Worcestershire in pre first-class days (just as Albert did) not to mention cousins Jim Windridge, a double sportsman with 12 first-class appearances for Warwickshire and who played soccer for Birmingham City (scoring twice on his debut), Chelsea and Middlesbrough and Albert Leake, who played soccer for Aston Villa and five times for England. Birmingham-born Albert bowled slow right-arm for Walsall in the Birmingham League and for Cadbury's, Bournville and made his debut in that first game against Yorkshire in 1899. During a 143 match Worcestershire career he took 292 wickets with a Championship best of 7-53 against Hampshire at Southampton in 1901, followed by 7-56 in the second innings to help the County to a fourth consecutive win. His best batting was 64 not out, batting at number ten and sharing a partnership of 92 with Fred Wheldon (still a Worcestershire record for the ninth wicket against Lancashire). He died in Worcester in 1927 aged fifty-nine although, as with many professionals of that day, there was some doubt about his actual age.

Cricket Match. Played at Birmingham Date 2·3·4 1909

Worcestershire VERSUS Warwickshire

1st INNINGS OF Worcestershire

ORDER OF GOING IN	BATSMAN'S NAME	RUNS AS SCORED	HOW OUT	BOWLER'S NAME	TOTAL RUNS
1	W. L. Foster		L B W.	Santall	41
2	Bowley		ct. Lilley	Foster	9
3	Pearson		ct. Binnie		22
4	Arnold		not	out	200
5	Cuffe		ct. Lilley	Santall	5
6	W. B. Burns		Bowled	Baker	196
7	M. K. Foster		ct. Foster	Santall	39
8	G. H. Simpson-Hayward		not	out	14
9	H. G. Baker	Did not Bat.			
10	Hon. C. F. Lyttelton		Innings declared closed		
11	Bale				
BYES		LEG BYES	WIDE BALLS	NO BALLS	52
RUNS AT THE FALL OF EACH WICKET	1 FOR 18	2 FOR 78	3 FOR 78	4 FOR 83	5 FOR 476	6 FOR 551	7 FOR	8 FOR	9 FOR	10 FOR	**TOTAL** 578

Excerpt from the 1909 Worcestershire scorebook showing the County Championship record fifth-wicket partnership of 393 by Ted Arnold and William Burns against Warwickshire at Edgbaston, a record that remained until beaten by Mal Loye and David Ripley with 401 for Northamptonshire against Glamorgan in 1998.

Cricket Match. Played at Stourbridge Date 5·6·7 July 1909

Worcestershire VERSUS Kent.

1st INNINGS OF Kent

ORDER OF GOING IN	BATSMAN'S NAME	RUNS AS SCORED	HOW OUT	BOWLER'S NAME	TOTAL RUNS
1	E. W. Dillon		Bowled	W. B. Burns	0
2	Humphreys		ct. Burns	Cuffe	37
3	Seymour		Bowled	W. B. Burns	4
4	K. L. Hutchings		ct. Taylor	Cuffe	61
5	Woolley		ct. W. B. Foster	Arnold	185
6	Hardinge		L B W.	Arnold	30
7	J. H. W. Broughton		Bowled	Taylor	46
8	Fairservice		Bowled	Cuffe	1
9	Huish			Taylor	22
10	Blythe		ct. Cuffe		0
11	Fielder		not	out	112
BYES		LEG BYES	WIDE BALLS 4	NO BALLS	56
RUNS AT THE FALL OF EACH WICKET	1 FOR 0	2 FOR 4	3 FOR 107	4 FOR 133	5 FOR 181	6 FOR 192	7 FOR 276	8 FOR 320	9 FOR 320	10 FOR	**TOTAL** 555

Another copy from the 1909 scorebook showing the British last-wicket record of 235 by Frank Woolley and Arthur Fielder for Kent at Stourbridge. This was Fielder's only first-class hundred and was the fourth for Woolley (and a career best at the time) towards his final collection of 145.

Frank Chester joined Worcestershire in 1912 and seemed to have the world at his feet when he scored 115 not out at New Road against Somerset in 1913 at the age of seventeen. The life of this promising cricketer however was shattered at Salonika during July 1917 when he lost his right arm. In his 1956 autobiography he writes: 'my young heart was bursting with the desire to resume where I had left off, but on a bitter battle-ground overseas I met disaster. Not until I looked round the hospital ward and saw the suffering far greater than mine was I able to give any constructive consideration to the future'. And there was a future. He became a most respected first-class umpire in 1922 and stood in 48 Tests until retiring in 1955. The Association of Cricket Statisticians however found something strange about his date of birth and owners of *Wisden* for 1979 and 1980 will notice that it changes from 1896 to 1895 in the latter edition, making him eighteen at the time of that maiden century.

Dick Burrows began his seventeen season career with Worcestershire in that first first-class match at New Road against Yorkshire in 1899 and he and H.K. Foster were the only two from that side that re-appeared after the First World War. Dick added 14 wickets in six non-Championship matches in 1919 to bring his final tally of Worcestershire wickets to 894 with a career best of 8-48 in 1908 against Somerset at Taunton in 14.1 overs. Batting was never his strong point, although there were two centuries in his aggregate of 5,223 runs at 14.07, but he is best remembered for a ninth-wicket partnership, still a Worcestershire record, with John Cuffe. Missed on the boundary when he was 22, he went on to a career best 112 with 19 fours and he and Cuffe added 181 at New Road against Gloucestershire. There must have been a keen fellow with a tape measure at Old Trafford in the early 1900s for, when Burrows bowled Archie MacLaren in 1901, a bail allegedly travelled 64 yards and 6 inches, a record at the time, only for him to return in 1911 and beat his own record with a bail this time travelling 67 yards 6 inches when he bowled Bill Huddleston.

Two
Between the Wars

Don Bradman made his first visit to New Road in 1930, then a twenty-one year old, and plundered the Worcestershire bowling for 236 runs. His next two visits were of similar nature with 206 in 1934 and 258 in 1938 (on which occasion he is pictured here). When he returned after the Second World War Worcestershire had the measure of him when Peter Jackson bowled him for only 107! His New Road tally was 807 runs in four innings at an average of 201.75. Above, left to right: S.H. Martin, R. Howorth, J.S. Buller, H.G. Baldwin (umpire), Bradman, A.P. Singleton, C.H. Bull, C.L. Badcock, R.T.D. Perks

Worcestershire *v.* Lancashire at New Road, 1921. From left to right, back row: Fred Hunt (groundsman), Major C.V. Beresford (secretary), A.J. Powell, C.V. Tarbox, A.M. Carr, H.O. Hopkins, J.F. Toppin. Seated: H.L. Higgins, Colonel W.H. Taylor, F.A. Pearson, Major M.F.S. Jewell (captain), F.L. Bowley, H.A. Gilbert, M.K. Foster. Front: C.A. Preece. Worcestershire lost fifteen matches during that season, six of them, including this one, by an innings. Groundsman Hunt was persuaded to join Worcestershire from Kent in 1898 by Mr Foley and he stayed there until the end of the Second World War. He was also a moderate all-rounder, playing 53 matches between 1900 and 1923, but as a groundsman he had no superior and farmed the land that until recently was a petrol station. The story goes that many times he and his staff would have to clear the ground of sheep, cattle and horses before play could begin. Two great servants of Worcestershire made their debuts in 1921, one of them was 'Percy' Tarbox, pictured here, and the other was Fred Root who made his debut, following his move from Derbyshire, in the return match at Old Trafford.

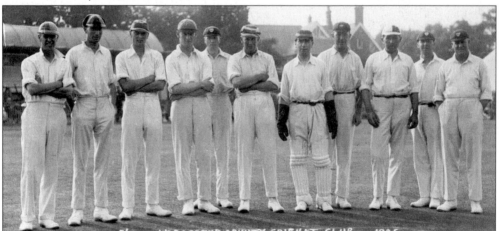

Worcestershire led by the youngest of the Foster brother, Maurice, in 1925 – another season that saw them languishing towards the foot of the County Championship table. Eighteen matches were lost, ten of them at home, and they won five. Foster played in every match and scored 1,453 runs, almost a thousand more than the next batsman, G.E.B. Abell, who scored 495.

M.F.S. Jewell first appeared for Worcestershire in 1909, playing just one match before moving to Sussex for the 1914 season. His tireless efforts got the club moving again after the war and he led the side in 1920 and for four more seasons during the twenties but with little success. Of the 72 times he led Worcestershire they won 10, lost 46 and drew 16, with their highest position in the Championship being fourteenth. He played his last match in 1933 and retired with 3,906 runs at 18.96 for Worcestershire and took 98 wickets at 32.82. The best of his two centuries, both scored in 1926, was 125 at New Road against Hampshire in the match that M.K. Foster scored 141 and 106. His brother, A.N., played 22 times for Worcestershire between 1919 and 1920 and his son, J.M.H., played twice in 1939. He married Elsie, the sister of another Worcestershire captain W.H. Taylor, in 1911 and they were married for over sixty years. During the First World War he served with the Royal Artillery as a Major commanding a battery in France. Jewell was elected club president in 1950 and held office until 1955. He was awarded the CBE and died, aged ninety-two, on 28 May 1978.

Maurice Jewell and the Australian captain, Warren Bardsley, go out for the toss in 1926. Charlie Macartney (5-38) and Clarrie Gimmett (4-2) bowled Worcestershire out in the first innings and Arthur Mailey (4-20) and Grimmett (4-31) in the second for an Australian win by 176 runs in two days.

'Dick' Pearson had a longer Worcestershire career than any other cricketer, having made his debut in May 1900 and finishing in September 1926. In 445 matches he scored 18,496 runs at 24.43, took 815 wickets at 29.65 and held 161 catches. Born in Brixton and initially turned down by the county of his birth, he must have quite enjoyed his hat-trick when he dismissed Andy Sandham, Percy Fender and William Abel at New Road, where he had figures of 6-55 against Surrey in 1914. His career-best bowling was also against Surrey when he took 8-42 at The Oval in 1907 and his best with the bat was 167 at Swansea when Worcestershire ventured into Wales for first-class cricket for the first time in 1921. In his autobiography Fred Root recalls him as being a fantastically unselfish player. At New Road in 1913 against Gloucestershire, Pearson and Bowley had an opening partnership of 306 in three-and-a-quarter hours with Pearson scoring 106 and Bowley 201. In 1923, at the age of almost forty-three, Pearson completed the double for Worcestershire with 1,052 runs and 111 wickets.

Maurice Jewell turns Tom Wall past wicketkeeper Bertie Oldfield during the opening over of the Australian Tour of 1930 at New Road. This match began a pattern that was to last until 1975 with the Australians playing their first first-class match of their tour in Worcester. Jewell was dismissed by Clarrie Grimmett for 7 and the Australians won by an innings and 165 runs with Don Bradman scoring 236, the first of his three double-centuries at New Road.

 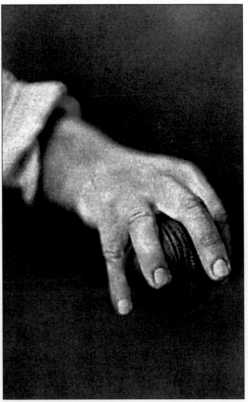

Left: Fred Root was born into cricket, being the son of the groundsman at Aylestone Road (then the headquarters of Leicestershire). He made his debut for Derbyshire, the county of his birth, in 1910 but joined Worcestershire in 1921 and until 1932 was the backbone of their bowling attack, taking 1,387 wickets at 20.52. In 1925 he took 207 first-class wickets for Worcestershire, including 27 five-wickets hauls (nine of which turned into ten in the match). Of the current county cricketers only Andy Caddick, with 11 ten-wickets in an innings, has taken more in a career, let alone a season! Despite this record he was rewarded with only three Test caps, the first at Trent Bridge against Australia in 1926 where there was only 50 minutes play and he didn't bat or bowl, the second at Lord's were he bowled Herbie Collins and had Bill Woodfull caught behind by Herbert Strudwick and the third at Old Trafford were he had his best figures of 4-84 in another rain-affected match. At the age of thirty-eight he completed his only 1,000 runs and 100 wickets double over the season of his only century in 1928. After his playing days were over he was on the umpires list in 1947 and 1948, coached Leicestershire in 1949 and 1950 and became a well-respected sports journalist. He wrote *A Cricket Pro's Lot* in 1937, a copy of which should be in every cricketer's bag to show them how lucky they are with their sponsored cars and six-figure benefit cheques. Root died in the Royal Hospital, Wolverhampton in 1954 aged sixty-three. *Right:* Bowling arm: Maurice Foster encouraged Root to bowl 'leg-theory', bowling fast-medium in-swingers on the leg stump with fieldsmen placed on the leg-side close to the batsmen.

Maurice Foster, sixth of the seven brothers, last appeared for Worcestershire in 1934 stretching the Worcestershire brotherhood to a spread of thirty-five seasons. Another Malvern Schoolboy, he made his debut against Lancashire in 1908, aged eighteen, scoring 20 at New Road. After his last match against Somerset in 1934, in which he captained the County in the absence of Cyril Walters, he had scored 7,876 runs at an average of 29.38 with 12 hundreds. The best of these was 158, at New Road in the last match before the First World War. M.K. didn't become a regular in the Worcestershire side until after the war, spending much of his time as a rubber planter in Malaya, but on his return he captained the side between 1923 and 1925. Like his brothers he excelled at other sports and played golf at an high standard and had a spell as captain of Walsall from 1932 until 1940 in the Birmingham League. During ARP duties he caught a chill after a Coventry air raid and died less than two months later on 3 December, aged fifty-one.

Worcestershire *v.* Gloucestershire at New Road, the last match of the 1927 season and another defeat, this time by nine wickets. From left to right, back row: H.H.I.H. Gibbons, W.V. Fox, H.O. Rogers, H. Williams, C.V. Tarbox, J.W. King. Front row: C.F. Root, J.B. Higgins, Hon C.B. Ponsonby (captain), H.O. Hopkins, A.F. Lane. This was the seventeenth defeat of the season and with only one win (by six wickets against Middlesex) Worcestershire finished at the foot of the County Championship table. Thirty-five players were used during the season, twenty-four of them amateurs, and many of them were found lacking.

Durham-born Maurice Nichol scored a century on his debut in 1928 against the West Indians at New Road. He hit 104 and shared a second-wicket partnership of 207 with Gibbons, who went on to score 200 not out. During his first full season of 1929 he made 1,442 runs in the Championship with two centuries, 132 at Dudley against Warwickshire and 137 at Bournemouth against Hampshire. Bournemouth was the venue again in 1930 when he had a career best 262 not out in five hours, with 33 fours, and a 90 minute fifth-wicket partnership of 130 with Vic Fox. Selection as twelfth man for England at Lord's against New Zealand followed in 1931 but during the winter of 1931/32 he spent several weeks in Sunderland Royal Infirmary where he was very seriously ill with pneumonia. A poor season followed but he was back to form in 1933, scoring over 2,000 runs including eight centuries, although he was taken ill at Leyton and was absent in the second innings and missed the home game with Derbyshire. Nichol began the 1934 season but, by a terribly strange coincidence in the match against Essex (this time at Chelmsford), after a tiring day in the Whit-Monday sun fielding to a total of 469, Nichol was found dead in his hotel bed the following morning at the early age of twenty-eight years old.

Scottish-born 'Peter' Jackson (christened Percy Frederick but always known as Peter), made his debut for Worcestershire against Lancashire in 1929. An off-spinner who regularly opened the attack with his medium-pacers, he took 1,159 wickets in a career that ended in 1950 having played 383 (out of a total of 385) of his first-class matches for Worcestershire, the odd two having been at the Harrogate Festival in 1947. On Saturday 11 May 1935, his twenty-fourth birthday, 25 wickets fell on the first day of the match against Middlesex at Lord's and Jackson, bowling round the wicket, took eight of them – seven bowled and one leg-before – for 64 runs and took another four – one bowled and three leg-before – in the second to finish with match figures of 12-119. Later that season he had career best figures of 9-45 when he bowled Somerset to a 173 runs defeat at Dudley, having taken 4-68 in their first innings. He took 100 wickets in a season four times for Worcestershire and at Neath in 1936 performed the hat-trick when he dismissed Dai Davies, George Lavis and Arthur Porter with consecutive deliveries. He took 194 catches, most of them at short leg without an helmet, and at the time of his death in May 1999 was the oldest living Worcestershire cricketer.

The Worcestershire side for the opening match of the season in 1931 at New Road where Northamptonshire were the visitors. They are, from left to right, standing: P.F. Jackson (twelfth man), M.E. White, L. Wright, R.T.D. Perks, M. Nichol, J. Fox, H.H.I.H. Gibbons. Seated: T.L. Winwood, C.F. Root, C.F. Walters (captain), B.W. Quaife, G.W. Brook. The match was drawn with Gibbons (74), Fox (73) and Nichol (51) batting well in the first innings whilst White (5-34) in the first innings and Root (5-85) in the second took the bowling honours. George Brook, a slow-left arm spinner, was starting his second season with Worcestershire having taken 128 Championship wickets during his initial season. When he joined the club he took seven years off his age and was actually in his forty-second year when he made his first-class debut in 1930, having spent many years in the Yorkshire Leagues.

'Doc' Gibbons (born with the christian names of Harry Harold Ian Haywood) earned his nickname from the little black bag that was the home of his cricket kit. Having been born in Devon he had to serve a qualifying period during which time he played for Dudley in the Birmingham League, but soon made a niche in the Worcestershire records. At New Road, against Hampshire, in 1939 he scored unbeaten hundreds in both innings, 111 in the first and 100 in the second, a Worcestershire record until equalled by Graeme Hick at Abergavenny in 1990 with 252* and 100*.

The Worcestershire side at Kidderminster in 1933 where they were beaten by 10 wickets by Somerset. They are, from left to right, standing: J. Fox, G.W. Brook, E.H. Perry, R.T.D. Perks, C.H. Bull, P.F. Jackson, M. Nichol. Seated: L. Wright, B.W. Quaife, C.F. Walters (captain), The Nawab of Pataudi, H.H.I.H. Gibbons. Wicketkeeper Bernard Quaife played for Warwickshire from 1920 until 1926 and was the son of George, a Warwickshire legend who had scored almost 40,000 runs. He joined Worcestershire in 1928 as an amateur and made 271 appearances in a ten-season stay, accumulating 8,498 runs with three centuries. One of them, at New Road in 1931 against Middlesex, helped Worcestershire to a (then) record fourth-wicket partnership: Quaife scored 107 and with Gibbons (183) added 277 runs in four hours and ten minutes, which remained unbeaten until Alan Ormrod and Younis Ahmed shared 281 runs at Trent Bridge in 1979.

Reg Perks, seen here in his left-handed batting mode, hit the ball a long way and holds the record for Worcestershire for the most runs (8,484) without scoring a century. His best innings was 75 out of 84 added for the last wicket with 'Roly' Jenkins at Trent Bridge in 1938, hitting 4 sixes and 8 fours in 30 minutes. Perks, however, was better known for his fast right-arm bowling and his aggregate of 2,143 wickets is a Worcestershire record, 531 more than his nearest rival Norman Gifford – and Perks missed six seasons because of the Second World War! The best of his 140 five-wicket performances was 9-40 at Stourbridge against Glamorgan in 1939. He took 100 wickets in a season 15 times, another Worcestershire record, and performed the hat-trick twice, against Kent at Stourbridge in 1931 and Warwickshire at Edgbaston in 1933.

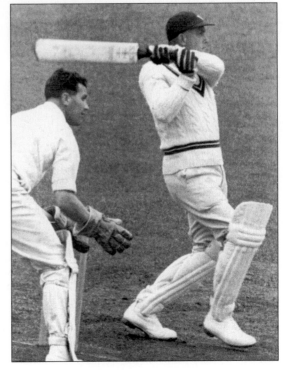

Perks made his Test debut in the longest ever first-class match that lasted ten days between 3 and 14 March 1939 (with two rest days) and would have continued had the MCC party not had to begin a two day train journey from Durban to catch their boat at Cape Town. He took 5-100 on his debut and made just one more appearance, against the West Indies at The Oval in 1939, where he took 5-156 in the last Test match before the war.

Worcestershire CCC, 1936. From left to right, back row: B.P. King, J.S. Buller, P.F. Jackson, S.H. Martin, F.B.T. Warne, R. Howorth. Middle row: H.H.I.H. Gibbons, B.W. Quaife, Hon. C.J. Lyttelton, R.H.C. Human, R.T.D. Perks. Front row: L. Oakley, C.H. Bull, A.P. Singleton, J. Horton, R.D.M. Evers. Charlie Bull met his death in a car crash on Whit-Sunday night in 1939 in the Chelmsford area and fellow passenger Syd Buller was injured. Bull scored five centuries in an eight season career and was also a good table tennis player, winning the English Open men's doubles championship with Fred Perry in 1928, 1929 and 1930. Buller, after his retirement, became a well-respected umpire and stood in 32 Test matches. In fact, he was standing in the match at Edgbaston between Warwickshire and Nottinghamshire in 1970 when he collapsed in the pavilion and died during a stoppage for rain.

Four Worcestershire bowlers who each took 100 wickets in 1937. From left to right: Reg Perks (139, av 20.59), Dick Howorth (105, av 24.94), 'Peter' Jackson (102, av 25.91) and Sid Martin (114, av 20.25). South African born Martin joined Worcestershire in 1931 after first-class experience with Natal in his homeland. He completed the 1,000 runs/100 wickets double twice for Worcestershire in 1937 and 1939, leaving when only 7 runs short of 10,000 having taken 459 wickets. At New Road in August 1935 he batted for 280 minutes, hit 4 sixes, a five and 19 fours in a career best 191 not out against Northamptonshire. During his last season in 1939 he had career best figures of 8-24 (13-88 in the match) at New Road against Sussex. Martin returned to South Africa and Natal until 1947 and then had three seasons with Rhodesia. His nephew was Hugh Tayfield, the brilliant South African off-spinner, and his son, Hugh, made five appearances for Transvaal and five for New South Wales, having made appearances for Worcestershire seconds in 1966. Martin went into cricket administration as Secretary of the Transvaal Cricket Union and the South African Cricket Association between 1969 and 1972.

Dick Howorth was another of the Worcestershire cricketers who suffered from those missing six seasons during the war and in the last match of the 1939 season he took the last Nottinghamshire wicket – Harold Butler caught by Charles Lyttelton – for his 100th wicket and so completed his first 1,000 runs/100 wickets double. Two more doubles followed immediately after the war and he made his Test debut in 1947, celebrating it with the wicket of Dennis Dyer, caught by Cliff Gladwin, off the first ball he bowled. Howorth was the second Worcestershire cricketer to achieve this following Ted Arnold, who dismissed Victor Trumper off his first ball in Test cricket at Sydney in December 1903. When he retired at the end of the 1951 season he had scored 10,538 runs and taken 1,274 wickets for Worcestershire, hit 3 centuries and had 71 five-wicket performances (turning seven of them into ten wickets in a match). The best of his centuries was his first at The Crabble, Dover in 1936 when he scored 114 against Kent. His best bowling return was 7-18 against Northamptonshire. At Edgbaston in 1950 he dismissed Tom Pritchard, Eric Hollies and Roly Thompson with consecutive balls for his only first-class hat-trick.

Worcestershire in 1938. From left to right, back row: P.F. Jackson (twelfth man), F.B.T. Warne, S.H. Martin, C.H. Bull, J.S. Buller, E. Cooper. Middle row: H.H.I.H. Gibbons, R.J. Crisp, Hon. C.J. Lyttelton (captain), R.T.D. Perks, R. Howorth. Front row: B.P. King, J. Horton. This was the team that beat Sussex by four wickets at New Road in early May after they had entertained Don Bradman (258) and the Australians for their tour opener. Charlie Bull was missing from this Sussex game, owing to a blow over the right eye that he received when trying to hook one of the many no-balls bowled by Ernie McCormick. When Bob Crisp joined Worcestershire for the 1938 season he had already played all his nine Tests for South Africa, and injury limited him to just eight matches. In those matches his fast bowling earned him five performances of five wickets in an innings with the best of them at Lord's when he had figures of 7-82 in a Middlesex total of 241.

'Roly' Jenkins, Worcestershire's most successful leg-spinner with 1,148 wickets from his debut in 1938 until his retirement in 1958. He performed three hat-tricks in his career, all of them against Surrey, including one in each innings at New Road in 1949. The double was performed twice by Jenkins in all matches in 1949 and 1952, but neither of these were solely for Worcestershire. He made nine Test appearances in total, five of them (including his debut) being in South Africa and four in England.

Charlie Palmer made his debut against Yorkshire in 1938 at Bradford but rain on the last two days meant that not even a result on the first innings could be achieved. At the time he was nineteen years old and studying at Birmingham University as he intended to go into the teaching profession, which he did for a short period. His maiden century, 132 at Dudley against Northamptonshire, was followed by another (128) in the next match at Cardiff. Again at Dudley in 1947, he produced his highest score for Worcestershire with 177 against Nottinghamshire, hitting 21 fours and sharing a second-wicket partnership of 128 with Don Kenyon and one of 138 with 'Roly' Jenkins for the sixth. Joe Hardstaff junior scored a double-century for the visitors in that match. Palmer impressed Don Bradman's Australians on their opening match of the 1948 tour, scoring 85, but his time with Worcestershire was short-lived and he became secretary of Leicestershire in 1950, continuing his playing career with them and winning his only Test cap in the West Indies when he was player/manager of the MCC party in 1953/54. He was elected Leicestershire president in 1987, was president of the MCC in 1978 and 1979 and returns every summer to New Road for the Worcestershire Old Players Association get-together.

Worcestershire CCC, 1939. From left to right, standing: H. Yarnold, B.P. King, E. Cooper, S.H. Martin, J.S. Buller, R.O. Jenkins, H.H.I.H. Gibbons. Seated: R. Howorth, A.F.T. White, C.J. Lyttelton (captain), R.T.D. Perks, C.H. Bull.

Three
The Kenyon Era

Don Kenyon made his debut for
Worcestershire in 1946. He was captain of
the county from 1959 until 1967, during
which time Worcestershire won their first
County Championship title in 1964 with a
repeat performance the following season.

'Sandy' Singleton, the first Worcestershire captain after the Second World War, made his first-class debut for Oxford University in 1934 and won his Blue that season and the three following seasons, captaining the side in 1937. His first Worcestershire appearance was also in 1934 and he finished his first season with a modest 144 runs at 28.80 and with 6 wickets from his off-breaks. He didn't appear at all for Worcestershire in 1937 and was not a regular member of the side until 1946. By the outbreak of war had played only 35 matches in six seasons but had scored his maiden century with 102 not out at New Road against Nottinghamshire in the last match of 1939. He scored three more centuries during his single season reign as captain, including a career best 164 at Edgbaston in three and a half hours, sharing partnerships of 126 for the first wicket with Eddie Cooper and 141 for the second with Ronnie Bird to help Worcestershire achieve their first double over neighbours Warwickshire since 1903. During the war he was a flying instructor in Rhodesia, met his future wife and settled there in 1947, farming and playing for Rhodesia until the end of the 1949/50 season. He made a return to New Road, with his brother, for the Worcestershire Old Players reunion on 21 August 1993. Singleton spent his final days in Australia where he died, aged eighty-six, in 1999.

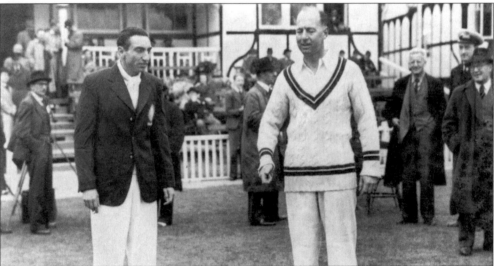

Singleton tosses the coin and the Nawab of Pataudi calls correctly, asking Worcestershire to bat in front of an estimated record crowd of 8,000 shivering spectators in May 1946. Pataudi scored 2,860 runs for Worcestershire in 37 matches between 1932 and 1938, turning eight of his centuries into double-centuries. Three of these double hundreds were scored in 1933 and two of them in consecutive matches: 231 (his highest score) at New Road against Essex and 222 at Weston-super-Mare against Somerset. He was a member of the infamous Douglas Jardine 1932/33 'bodyline series' touring party in Australia, playing in the first two Tests. He adding another cap at Trent Bridge against the 1934 Australians and made his Test debut for India at Lord's in June 1946. He was followed into the Indian side by his son, Mansur Ali Khan, who played in 46 Tests between 1961 and 1975.

Worcestershire assembled ready to secure the only win by a county side against the 1947 South African tourists. From left to right, standing: F. Cooper, D. Kenyon, E. Cooper, R. Howorth, R.O. Jenkins, H. Yarnold. Front row: R.T.D. Perks, R.E. Bird, A.F.T. White (captain), R.E.S. Wyatt, P.F. Jackson. Kenyon was making his first appearance since leaving the RAF and Fred Copper (brother of Eddie) was making his Worcestershire debut following his move from Lancashire. Former Warwickshire and England captain Bob Wyatt, who was in his second season at New Road, shared the captaincy with Alan White in 1949 and was appointed captain for 1950 and 1951, with Ronnie Bird taking over in 1952. White was also a former Warwickshire cricketer, making nine appearances between 1936 and 1937 and winning a Blue for Cambridge University in 1936.

Eddie Cooper plays on to Athol Rowan in the match against the 1947 South Africans in the first innings; this meant that the first Cooper brothers partnership was all over with the score at 19. However, later in the season at New Road they had an opening stand of 163 against Essex with Eddie scoring 84 and Fred 73. Fred, the younger of the brothers, left at the end of the 1950 season, having scored 1,204 in 39 matches at 19.11, reaching three figures once. At Trent Bridge in 1948 he scored 113 not out to save the match against Nottinghamshire, sharing a second-wicket partnership of 180 with 'Roly' Jenkins who hit 109. Brother Eddie had scored exactly 100 in four hours and forty minutes in the first innings. In later life Fred was in local government and at one point was chairman of the Wyre Forest Council in Worcestershire. He outlived his brother by eighteen years and died, aged sixty-five, in 1986.

Don Kenyon's first regular opening partner was Eddie Cooper and they shared fifteen century partnerships (fourteen of them for the first wicket) with a best of 197 at New Road against Derbyshire in 1951. Cooper scored 92 and Kenyon was 100 not out in a match that was troubled by rain.

'Laddie' Outschoorn was born in Ceylon and qualified for Worcestershire after playing for Kidderminster in the Birmingham League, having spent three and a half years in a Japanese prisoner of war camp after being captured whilst working in Malaya. He made his Worcestershire debut in 1946 against the Combined Services and his Championship debut the following season, scoring 62 not out at New Road against Gloucestershire. Later in the season he celebrated the award of his County Cap with a splendid performance by taking five catches in the Derbyshire first innings and scoring his maiden century (100 not out) in Worcestershire's second innings, just failing to clinch a five-wicket win with only 5 runs required when time ran out. His fielding at slip and gully was an inspiration and in 1949 he held onto 55 catches (he had a total of 276 in his career). The best of his 25 hundreds was 215 not out, including 2 sixes and 18 fours, against Northamptonshire at New Road and he shared a 241 partnership for the third wicket with Charlie Palmer (136), which was the highest at the time for Worcestershire since the war. In 1966 he became Ceylon's national coach and died in London in 1994 aged seventy-five.

This is the Worcestershire team that welcomed Don Bradman's all-conquering side of 1948. From left to right, standing: H. Yarnold, R.O. Jenkins, D. Kenyon, R. Howorth, E. Cooper, L.F. Outschoorn. Seated: P.F. Jackson, R.E.S. Wyatt, A.F.T. White, C.H. Palmer, R.T.D. Perks. Note that Wyatt, Perks and Howorth are proudly wearing their MCC touring blazers. Worcestershire batted first and Ray Lindwall had Don Kenyon leg-before for 0 with the second ball of the match, but a second-wicket partnership of 137 between Eddie Cooper and Charlie Palmer helped them to a respectable 233 total. Bradman followed his three double-centuries on his previous visits with a modest 107, being overshadowed by Arthur Morris who scored 138 on his first appearance in England. The Australian pair added 186 for the second wicket and the tourists declared on 462-8 before bowling Worcestershire to an innings and 17 runs defeat. An estimated crowd of 32,000 watched the three day's play with receipts of over £4,000, a club record at the time.

Don Kenyon sweeps Jack Hill, during the Australians' visit to New Road in 1953, on his way to his 122. He became the first batsman to score a century for Worcestershire against the Australians and hit 13 fours. However, his innings was dwarfed by a massive 220 not out by Keith Miller, who hit a six and 18 fours in six and a quarter hours.

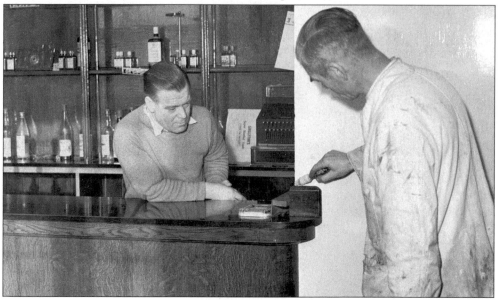

Hugo Yarnold supervises the decoration of the bar of the Royal George in Worcester during the 1950s. Yarnold kept wicket for Worcestershire following the Second World War, when Syd Buller retired. He took 685 dismissals in 283 matches, including seven in an innings against Scotland at Dundee in 1951 (with a world record six stumpings). During the 1949 season he had an aggregate of 104 dismissals (60 caught and 44 stumped).

'Roly' Jenkins takes his daughter for a walk and, as ever, enjoys a smoke. It would be hard to find anyone who loved cricket as much as 'Roly', who was always willing to talk for any cricket society and was well known for helping young cricketers.

Worcestershire once again inflicted the only defeat on the South Africans by an county side, this time on their 1955 tour. From left to right, standing: L.F. Outschoorn, R.G. Broadbent, J.P. Whitehead, J.A. Flavell, M.J. Horton, G. Dews, R. Berry. Seated: D. Kenyon, P.E. Richardson, R.T.D. Perks (captain), R.O. Jenkins, H. Yarnold. Martin Horton's match-winning 9-56 in the South Africans' second innings were the best figures against the 1955 South Africans and he finished the game with 11-83. Reg Perks became the first professional to be officially appointed captain of Worcestershire in this match.

John Waite is bowled by Bob Berry in the first innings – one of Berry's 5-60. Berry was making his Worcestershire debut following 93 appearances for Lancashire between 1948 and 1954. In 1953 at Blackpool he took all ten Worcestershire wickets in their second innings for 102 to add to his first innings figures of 4-23. His career best figures for Worcestershire were 6-37 at Bristol against Gloucestershire in 1956 and he left to join Derbyshire in 1959, having taken 250 wickets at 25.05.

Peter Richardson and Don Kenyon go out to open the Worcestershire innings against the 1955 South Africans. The partnership was short-lived when Richardson was bowled by Peter Heine before he had scored with the total at 7. Peter was the eldest of the three Herefordshire Richardson brothers and scored 9,118 runs during his ten season with Worcestershire, before moving on to Kent in 1959. He played 34 Tests for England, scoring five centuries, but his career best was for Worcestershire when he scored 185 at Kidderminster against Somerset in 1954, hitting 19 fours.

Bob Broadbent joined Worcestershire in 1950 having previously played second eleven cricket for Middlesex after serving as a RAF navigator. He made an impressive debut with the bat in the last match of the 1950 season, with 77 and 29 not out against Leicestershire at Grace Road, but taking the new ball with Reg Perks he was hit for 26 off his first three overs (including eighteen off four balls struck by Les Berry). Broadbent was a dependable batsman who scored 12,800 runs for Worcestershire at 27.58 and an excellent close fielder. At Stourbridge in 1960 he held a Worcestershire record six catches against Glamorgan: three off Doug Slade, two off Jack Flavell and one off Martin Horton, having also taken one off Flavell in the first innings. The best of his fourteen centuries was against his former county, Middlesex, when he hit 155 at New Road in 1951 in five and a quarter hours (with 2 sixes and 22 fours) sharing hundred partnerships with Ronnie Bird and Eddie Cooper. Another of the many all-round sportsmen that have appeared for Worcestershire, he also represented the county at hockey

Worcestershire again played hosts for the first first-class appearance in England of the 1956 Australians. The home side consisted of, from left to right, standing: G. Dews, R. Booth, J.A. Flavell, R.G. Broadbent (twelfth man), D.W. Richardson, M.J. Horton, R. Berry. Seated: D. Kenyon, G.H. Chesterton, P.E. Richardson (captain), R.O. Jenkins, L.F.Outschoorn. This was Peter Richardson's first appearance as officially appointed captain following the retirement of Reg Perks and he played a match-saving innings of 130 not out when Worcestershire followed-on and held out for a draw, with last man Jack Flavell successfully facing the final three balls of the match.

Don Kenyon is bowled by Ray Lindwall for 21 in the first innings of the 1956 match against Australia. Worcestershire were all out for 90, George Dews top scoring with 31 and Ray Lindwall taking 3-22. Richie Benaud scored 160 in the Australians' innings, adding 126 for the sixth wicket with wicketkeeper Len Maddocks.

Don Kenyon took over the captaincy of Worcestershire when Peter Richardson left to join Kent in 1959. He is pictured here inspecting the wicket with groundsman Mike Biddle and secretary Joe Lister. Lister joined the club from Yorkshire in 1954 and played 21 matches for Worcestershire, with the unfortunate best score of 99 against Kent at New Road in 1955. He became secretary in 1956 (jointly with Peter Richardson for the first two years) and moved back to Yorkshire after the 1971 season.

Roy Booth, another import from Yorkshire, joined Worcestershire in 1956 and made his debut against the touring Australians at New Road. By the time he made the last of his 402 appearances in 1970 he had held 868 catches, taken 147 stumpings and scored 9,360 runs at 19.21. In 1964 he was the last wicketkeeper to take over 100 dismissals in a season, a performance he had also matched in 1960. The best of his two centuries was his maiden 113 not out at Hove against Sussex in 1959, hitting 16 fours and sharing a sixth-wicket partnership of 111 with 'Laddie' Outschoorn. However, the innings for which he will be most remembered was a modest 38, also at Hove – not only a match-winning score but (in partnership with Dick Richardson) one which helped Worcestershire to their second Championship title. Roy is amongst a number of Yorkshire-born wicketkeepers to play for Worcestershire, beginning with George Gaukrodger in 1900 and ending (at the moment) with Steven Rhodes and Jamie Pipe. Roy has a unique similarity with one of them: Syd Buller began his first-class career with Yorkshire and ended it with Worcestershire (as did Roy) and Syd's wife, Lillian, helped with the teas in the famous Ladies Pavilion, as did Roy's wife Joyce for several years. Roy was elected president in 1999, a position that he no doubt will serve with just as much distinction as he did behind the stumps.

Worcestershire at Scarborough in 1957. Although the weather looks fine in the picture, rain ruined the match with each side having just one innings each. The Worcestershire side are, from left to right: D.W. Richardson, R.G. Broadbent, L.J. Coldwell, G.H. Chesterton, M.J. Horton, R. Booth, J.A. Flavell, P.E. Richardson (captain), D. Kenyon, G. Dews, L.F. Outschoorn. England soccer and cricket double international Willie Watson scored 102 and shared a third-wicket partnership of 166 with Brian Close (who was himself a useful performer with the larger ball having been on the staffs of Arsenal, Leeds United and Bradford City). There were two useful footballers in the Worcestershire side as well, George Dews and Jack Flavell both played the game at professional level.

Fred Rumsey made his debut for Worcestershire in 1960, but with Flavell and Coldwell performing so well opportunities were rare and in three seasons he only made 13 appearances before moving on to Somerset where he achieved greater success. Whilst with Worcestershire he took 31 wickets at 21.32 (with a best of 7-50 at Chesterfield against Derbyshire in 1962) and took 11-96 in his last match for the county. During his time with Somerset he won five Test caps, the first at Old Trafford where Bobby Simpson made 311 and the Australian first wicket didn't fall until there were 201 runs on the board. His best Test figures were 4-25 at Lord's against the 1965 New Zealanders and on leaving Somerset after 153 matches he joined Derbyshire as their public relations officer and played mostly one-day cricket for them. He left Derbyshire to begin a successful cricket holiday business.

Worcestershire openers Don Kenyon and Peter Richardson shared twenty-two century opening partnerships, the first one being 116 against Essex at Romford in 1952 and the last 155, also against Essex but this time at New Road, in 1955. Their best partnership took place at Dudley against Gloucestershire in 1953 when, in just under five hours, they added 290 runs with Kenyon scoring 151 and Richardson 148. They were 19 runs short of the club's best first-wicket stand by H.K. Foster and F.L. Bowley at Derby in 1901 when Kenyon was caught behind off Tom Graveney.

Above: Martin Horton receives coaching from Surrey and England off-spinner Jim Laker. Horton, a Worcester born cricketer, gave his county sterling service, becoming a regular opening batsman and a more-than-useful off-spinner. *Below*: Horton at the crease. Martin made his debut in 1952, having first joined the county as a fifteen year old in 1949 (and in those days careers suffered from two or three years National Service). After a full season in 1953, when he scored 270 runs and took 27 wickets, he made just five appearances over the following two seasons. After he was demobbed he became a regular in the 1955 side, scoring 1,217 runs and taking 95 wickets for Worcestershire, and was awarded his County Cap. With the help of the Torquay Festival in September he increased his

wickets tally to over 100 with figures of 6-170 and 2-37 for the North against the South to become the last Worcestershire cricketer to complete the 1,000 runs and 100 wickets double in a season. The best of his 22 centuries for the club was 233 at Worcester against Somerset in 1962, hitting 36 fours in four and three quarter hours – sharing an opening partnership of 167 with Kenyon. The best was yet to come when Tom Graveney joined Martin for a Worcestershire record partnership for the third wicket of 314, a record that stood until 1997. The nearest he got to the match double of one hundred runs and ten wickets was 78 and 29 with the bat and 3-55 and 6-88 with the ball at Oxford against the University in 1962. His best figures were 9-56 against the 1955 South Africans and his best figures were a match-winning performance of 6-38 and 7-29 at Bath in 1956 in a low scoring game against Somerset. During the second innings of this match he performed his only hat-trick when he dismissed Harold Stephenson, Maurice Tremlett and Graham Atkinson with consecutive deliveries. Martin is currently the chairman of Worcestershire and president of the Stourbridge Cricket Society.

Kent v Worcestershire at The Nevill Ground, Tunbridge Wells, 15th June 1960

Kent won the toss and chose to field

Kent   1st Innings

```
P.E.Richardson                b Flavell      23
A.H.Phebey                    b Gifford      16
*M.C.Cowdrey    c Broadbent   b Pearson      17
R.C.Wilson      c Headley     b Flavell       0
S.E.Leary       st Booth      b Slade        23
P.H.Jones       c Broadbent   b Slade        73
A.L.Dixon       c Dews        b Pearson      17
+A.W.Catt       st Booth      b Gifford       0
D.J.Halfyard    st Booth      b Gifford       0
A.Brown                       b Gifford       1
P.A.Shenton         not           out         7
     Extras            (b 7, lb 2, nb 1)     10
                                            ---
     TOTAL                                   187
```

```
Flavell    18    8    25    2       1- 41
Pearson    16    7    35    2       2- 43
Slade      18    5    54    2       3- 43
Gifford    17    5    63    4       4- 68
                                    5-104
                                    6-151
                                    7-154
                                    8-161
                                    9-179
                                   10-187
```

Worcestershire   1st Innings   2nd Innings

```
R.G.A.Headley              b Halfyard    0     c Wilson      b Halfyard     0
J.B.Sedgley c Leary        b Brown       7     c Richardson  b Brown        2
A.H.Spencer               b Brown       0     c Leary       b Brown        4
D.W.Richardson             b Brown       0                   b Halfyard     2
R.G.Broadbent              b Halfyard    0     c Catt        b Halfyard    22
* G.Dews        lbw        b Brown       0                   b Brown        0
+ R.Booth                  b Brown       2     c Shenton     b Halfyard     7
D.N.F.Slade                b Halfyard    9     c Leary       b Shenton     11
N.Gifford       not            out       0     c Brown       b Shenton      4
D.B.Pearson                b Halfyard    0     c Cowdrey     b Halfyard     2
J.A.Flavell                b Brown       1         not           out        0
     Extras          (b 1, lb 5)        6          (b 5, lb 1, w 1)        7
                                       ---                                ---
     TOTAL                               25                                61
```

```
Halfyard    9    4    7    4     1- 6     13    4    20    5      1- 0
Brown     8.1    5   12    6     2- 7      8    2    22    3      2- 6
Shenton                          3- 8    4.5    0    12    2      3- 7
                                 4- 9                             4- 17
                                 5- 9                             5- 18
                                 6- 9                             6- 40
                                 7- 24                            7- 51
                                 8- 24                            8- 51
                                 9- 24                            9- 61
                                10- 25                           10- 61
```

Kent won by an innings and 101 runs

Umpires : T.J.Bartley and J.S.Buller

Kent *v.* Worcestershire scorecard, 1960. This match was Norman Gifford's first-class debut and he bowled Arthur Phebey with the third ball of his first over. The match was the last to finish in a day in the world and the first in England since 1953. The pitch was described by Colin Cowdrey as being 'disgraceful' and the fixture was over by 7.15 p.m. on the Wednesday evening. Worcestershire's first innings had lasted 95 minutes and the second 100.

The Worcestershire side that entertained Richie Benaud's Australians for the first match of 1961. From left to right: N. Gifford, R.G.A. Headley, D.B. Pearson, T.E. Davies (twelfth man), L.J. Coldwell, R. Booth. Seated: M.J. Horton, G. .Dews, D. Kenyon (captain), J.A. Flavell, T.W. Graveney, D.W. Richardson. This was Tom Graveney's Worcestershire debut after moving from Gloucestershire; Kenyon won the toss and put the visitors in. Martin Horton took 5-46 in the first innings and Len Coldwell 5-45 in the second to put Worcestershire in a strong position but rain after lunch on the third day ended their chase on 56-4 with another 107 required for victory.

Norman Gifford, following his remarkable debut at Tunbridge Wells in 1960, adequately filled the gap left by Dick Howorth and during his first full season in 1961 he took over 100 wickets, a performance he repeated in 1964 and 1970. He took five wickets in an innings 76 times, turning twelve of them into ten-in-a-match performances. At Chesterfield in 1965 he dismissed Edwin Smith (stumped by Roy Booth), bowled Harold Rhodes and had Brian Jackson caught by Ron Headley off consecutive balls to complete the hat-trick and at Bramall Lane, Sheffield in 1968 he had career best figures of 8-28 against Yorkshire – but still finished on the losing side in a low-scoring match. All eight of the Yorkshire wickets belonged to Test cricketers and he took another four wickets in the second innings before the home side won by six wickets with Ray Illingworth, one of his eight victims, having match figures of 10-79. Gifford was around at the same time as Don Wilson and Derek Underwood and, but for these two left-armers, would probably have made more than his 15 Test appearances. Norman never gave his wicket away easily and this was emphasised by an innings at New Road in 1979. With the score at 80-6 at tea on the last day against Sussex, chasing a total of 255, Norman played a true captain's innings, scoring 1 not out in 98 minutes during which time 42 overs were bowled. By the time he left Worcestershire at the end of the 1982 season he had taken 1,615 wickets for Worcestershire, an aggregate beaten only by Reg Perks.

Jack Flavell came into the Worcestershire side in 1949 when Reg Perks was still playing and at the time of his retirement in 1967 was sharing the new ball with Len Coldwell. He took 1,507 wickets for the county, with a best of 9-30 at The Crabble, Dover in 1955 (one of his 86 five-wickets-in-an-innings performances), and was selected for four Test Matches.

Worcestershire in 1962 at The Oval. From left to right, standing: J.A. Standen, R.G.M. Carter, L.J. Coldwell, N. Gifford, D.N.F. Slade, J.A. Ormrod. Seated: R. Booth, R.G. Broadbent, D. Kenyon (captain), M.J. Horton, D.W. Richardson. Rain ruined this match with just 44 overs bowled on the first day and none on the second. Surrey took the bonus points with their first-innings lead after Roy Booth (43) had top scored for Worcestershire.

Martin Horton receives the Man of the Match award from Herbert Sutcliffe for his 51 and 2-20 (off 10 overs) against Essex at New Road in 1966.

Left-hander Ron Headley, son of the great George, hit 32 hundreds for Worcestershire, the best of them being 187 at New Road against Northamptonshire in 1971, adding 125 for the first wicket with Peter Stimpson. He hit another hundred in the second innings (108) and shared another opening partnership with Stimpson of 147. The first of his two Test appearances for the West Indies was at The Oval in 1973, where he scored 42 in the second innings before being bowled by Geoff Arnold.

Worcestershire Second XI against Kent at New Road in 1966. From left to right, standing: A.R. Barker, D. Isles, K.R. Baylis, T.J. Yardley, W.J. Beel, H. Martin, P.C. Birtwistle, E.J.O. Hemsley, W.G. Parkhouse (coach). Seated: L.J. Coldwell, J.A. Standen, J. Lister (secretary), D.N. Fearnely, D.N.F. Slade. 'Len' Beel played in goal for Birmingham City once in 1965 at St Andrews in a 5-5 draw with Blackburn Rovers and played one Sunday League match for Somerset in 1969. Gilbert Parkhouse is the former Glamorgan and England batsman and Hugh Martin is the son of Worcestershire's Sid.

Four bowlers repeated the performance of the 1937 quartet by each taking over 100 wickets in the 1961 season. From left to right: Martin Horton (101 at 21.12), Len Coldwell (140 at 19.25), Norman Gifford (133 at 19.66) and Jack Flavell (158 at 17.21). Flavell finished at the top of the national bowling averages and Worcestershire finished in fourth place in the Championship.

Len Coldwell played Minor Counties cricket for Devon (the county of his birth) in 1953 and 1954, joining Worcestershire in 1955. He had taken 1,029 wickets by the time he retired at the end of the 1969 season, with a career best of 8-38 against Surrey at New Road in 1965. In 1957 at Stourbridge he did the hat-trick against Leicestershire, dismissing Jack Firth, John Savage and Ray Smith. He repeated the feat against Essex at Brentwood in 1965 when he dismissed Keith Fletcher, Geoffrey Smith and Brian Taylor.

Tom Graveney cover drives to the boundary. Graveney, one of the best exponents of this shot since the Second World War, made his debut for Gloucestershire in 1948 and, after a disagreement over the captaincy, left to join Worcestershire, spending a qualifying period in the Birmingham League with Dudley. His 13,160 runs at 46.17 for Worcestershire came in ten seasons from 1961 and he hit 27 centuries, including his 100th in first-class cricket. After the retirement of Don Kenyon he captained Worcestershire between 1968 and 1970 and twenty-four years later was elected president of the club.

Doug Slade shared slow left-arm bowling duties with Norman Gifford in the sixties following his debut in 1958. He took 469 wickets at 22.94 with a career best performance of 7-47 at Lord's against Middlesex in 1970, finishing with 11-79 in the match. Many thought that Slade should have batted higher up the order than he did. His only century was at Grace Road in 1969 against Leicestershire when he scored 125, coming in as night-watchman after Ron Headley had been bowled for 0 by Graham McKenzie. After the dismissal of Rodney Cass and Alan Ormrod, Slade shared a partnership of 133 for the fourth wicket with Tom Graveney at a run a minute – his innings included 20 fours and took three and three-quarter hours – until he was caught by Micky Norman off Roy Barratt. When he retired after his benefit season in 1971 he joined West Bromwich Dartmouth in the Birmingham League. In 1960, aged nineteen years old, he had made his debut in that competition for Stourbridge with 8-35 against Dudley. Eighteen years later he broke the record for most runs in a season in the League with 1,407, an aggregate that included a record seven centuries. During this period he played Minor Counties cricket for Shropshire, captaining them in 1977 and 1978 and scoring 3,322 runs, with eight centuries, and taking 151 wickets. Slade was on the Worcestershire committee from 1979 until 1992 and was made a vice-president in 1993.

The Don Kenyon era ended against Glamorgan at Colwyn Bay on 1 September 1967. He won the toss and chose to bat, but was bowled third ball for 0 by Jeff Jones, doing much better in the second innings when he finished with 67 not out, sharing an unbroken second-wicket partnership of 111 with Alan Ormrod when time was called and the game was drawn. He left with 34,490 runs for Worcestershire, including 70 hundreds – the best of them 259 against Yorkshire at Kidderminster in 1956.

Don Kenyon plants a tree to commemorate his long Worcestershire career. Looking on are, from left to right: Revd Prebendary W.R. Chignell (Worcestershire historian), Jack Sellars and Gilbert Ashton. The dog's name has been lost in the mists of time!

Four
Champions!

Don Kenyon acknowledges the crowd at New Road following victory over Gloucestershire after their nearest rivals Warwickshire lost at Southampton. The County Championship was won by Worcestershire for the first time in 1964 with three games left. The side won 18 of their 28 matches

The Worcestershire staff that took the 1964 County Championship title. From left to right, standing: N. Gifford (26 CC apps), R.G.A. Headley (28), J.A. Ormrod (11), R.G.M. Carter (11), L.J. Coldwell (18), J.A. Standen (11), D.W. Richardson (26), D.N.F. Slade (19). Seated: R. Booth (28), T.W. Graveney (28), D. Kenyon (27), J.A. Flavell (19), M.J. Horton (28).

Don Kenyon with, from left to right: Norman Gifford, Len Coldwell, Roy Booth and Jack Flavell on the balcony after the defeat of Gloucestershire at New Road. Booth stumped Ken Graveney off Gifford when Gloucestershire, following-on, were just two runs away from making Worcestershire bat again.

WORCESTERSHIRE WIN THE 1964 CHAMPIONSHIP

Worcestershire v Gloucestershire at The County, Ground, New Raod, Worcester

22nd, 24th, 25th August 1964

Worcestershire won the toss and decided to bat

Worcestershire   1st Innings

• D.Kenyon		b Mortimore	114
M.J.Horton	c Meyer	b Windows	96
R.G.A.Headley	not	out	103
T.W.Graveney	c Windows	b Mortimore	57
D.W.Richardson	not	out	18
J.A.Ormrod			
✦ R.Booth			
N.Gifford			
B.M.Brain			
L.J.Coldwell			
J.A.Flavell			
Extras	(b 6, lb 3, w 0, nb 1)		10
TOTAL	(for 3 wkts dec)		398

Brown A.S.	29	3	121	0	1-187
Windows	15	2	58	1	2-223
Mortimore	39	10	89	2	3-349
Graveney	12	2	29	0	
Allen	24	5	91	0	

Gloucestershire   1st Innings   2nd Innings

	1st Innings			2nd Innings		
R.B.Nicholls	Ormrod	b Coldwell	7	lbw	b Flavell	22
✦ B.J.Meyer	c Headley	b Brain	25	c Booth	b Flavell	5
D.M.Young	c Kenyon	b Flavell	2	c Booth	b Gifford	10
D.W.Brown	c Headley	b Flavell	0		b Brain	0
M.G.Bevan	lbw	b Flavell	0	not	out	8
A.S.Brown	c Horton	b Gifford	21	c Booth	b Flavell	18
D.A.Allen	c Graveney	b Gifford	22	lbw	b Gifford	68
R.C.White		b Gifford	12	run out		21
J.B.Mortimore	c Graveney	b Flavell	47		b Gifford	9
A.R.Windows		b Brain	28	c Richardson	b Brain	1
• J.K.Graveney	not	out	19	st Booth	b Gifford	19
Extras	(b 3, lb 5, nb 1)		9	(b 13, lb 7, nb 3)		23
TOTAL			192			204

Flavell	20.3	5	44	4	1- 25	26	3	69	3	1- 22
Coldwell	20	11	14	1	2- 28	6	4	9	0	2- 23
Brain	17	4	52	2	3- 28	12	0	32	2	3- 31
Gifford	24	8	61	3	4- 28	32.2	15	50	4	4- 56
Horton	7	4	12	0	5- 50	10	2	21	0	5- 71
					6- 64					6- 77
					7- 86					7-171
					8- 95					8-172
					9-148					9-179
					10-192					10-204

Worcestershire won by an innings and 2 runs

Umpires : F.Jakeman and W.E.Phillipson

Worcestershire *v.* Gloucestershire scorecard. Kenyon and Horton's 187-run partnership for Worcestershire's first wicket was the best of the summer for any wicket and later Headley and Graveney added 126 for the third. Kenyon, first out, hit a six and 11 fours in three and a half hours and Headley's 103, with 2 sixes and 14 fours, took two and a half hours. More than 1,000 supporters waited to hear the result from Southampton which, when Warwickshire were beaten, meant that Worcestershire had won the County Championship for the first time.

Celebrations in the dressing room after the news from Southampton in 1964. From left to right, back: Martin Horton, Alan Ormrod. Front: Roy Booth, Norman Gifford, Ron Headley, Jack Flavell, Tom Graveney, Dick Richardson, Don Kenyon.

Duncan Fearnley turns the ball past Yorkshire wicketkeeper Jimmy Binks, with Ron Headley at the other end, during a 92-run defeat at Scarborough in 1964. Worcestershire were going through a sticky period having lost to Somerset and drawn with Essex. This defeat against Yorkshire followed losing to Hampshire – all in eleven July days. Fortunately, they won eight of their next ten games with the other two being drawn. Fearnley made 22 appearances in the 1964 side and, in a Worcestershire career that began in 1962, he scored 3,294 runs at 11.10 with a career best 112 at Kidderminster against Derbyshire in 1966. After leaving the club he played Minor Counties cricket for Lincolnshire before returning to captain the second eleven in 1972 whilst building a successful cricket bat manufacturing business. He was chairman between 1986 and 1998 and at the helm when two Championships, two Sunday Leagues, a NatWest Trophy and a Benson & Hedges Cup were won.

The Worcestershire balcony at Hove as Dick Richardson and Roy Booth add 51 for the sixth wicket in their second innings against Sussex. Booth was out shortly after this photograph was taken and Richardson, who batted two and a half hours for his 31, stayed to see Worcestershire to a four-wicket victory, thus retaining the Championship title in their centenary year. The players in the picture are, from left to right: Alan Ormrod, Ron Headley, Jack Flavell, Don Kenyon and Doug Slade (who went in after the dismissal of Booth).

Bath time at Hove. From left to right: Roy Booth, Jack Flavell, Norman Gifford, Dick Richardson, Doug Slade and Len Coldwell. Gifford is helping to submerge Ron Headley (who is sensibly saving his pint from the same fate).

WORCESTERSHIRE RETAIN THE CHAMPIONSHIP TITLE

Sussex v Worcestershire at County Ground, Eaton Road, Hove

28th, 30th, 31st August 1965

Toss won by Worcestershire who chose to field.

Sussex	1st Innings				2nd Innings		
K.G.Suttle	lbw	b Flavell	15	c Richardson	b Flavell	14
J.Langridge	lbw	b Flavell	6	c Booth	b Coldwell	14
L.J.Lenham	c Booth	b Coldwell	3		b Gifford	11
*Nawab of Pataudi jn	lbw	b Coldwell	3	c Booth	b Slade	60
G.C.Cooper	lbw	b Flavell	0		b Flavell	7
A.S.M.Oakman		b Flavell	0	c D'Oliveira	b Slade	12
P.J.Graves		b Flavell	0	c D'Oliveira	b Gifford	24
N.I.Thomson	c Booth	b Flavell	24	c Booth	b Gifford	30
A.Buss		b Flavell	7	c D'Oliveira	b Gifford	9
+ T.Gunn	not	out	0	not	out	19
J.A.Snow	st Booth	b Gifford	3		c & b Gifford	16
Extras	(b 4, lb 5, nb 2)		11	(b 4, lb 5, nb 0)		9
TOTAL			72			225

Flavell	13	4	26	7	1- 25	25	6	54	2	1- 17		
Coldwell	11	3	28	2	2- 26	13	2	42	1	2- 35		
D'Oliveira	3	1	5	0	3- 31					3- 61		
Gifford	4.4	2	2	1	4- 37	35	15	71	5	4- 77		
Slade					5- 37	21	8	49	2	5-105		
					6- 37					6-144		
					7- 37					7-178		
					8- 58					8-180		
					9- 69					9-189		
					10- 72					10-225		

Worcestershire	1st Innings				2nd Innings		
*D.Kenyon	c Gunn	b Snow	2	c Suttle	b Snow	21
R.G.A.Headley	c Gunn	b Buss	10	lbw	b Snow	0
J.A.Ormrod	c Gunn	b Thomson	13	c Langridge	b Snow	9
T.W.Graveney		b Oakman	49	c Langridge	b Snow	2
B.L.D'Oliveira	lbw	b Suttle	16	lbw	b Oakman	22
D.W.Richardson		b Thomson	41	not	out	31
+R.Booth		b Oakman	21	c Gunn	b Snow	38
D.N.F.Slade		b Oakman	4	not	out	5
N.Gifford	not	out	1			
L.J.Coldwell		b Thomson	0			
J.A.Flavell		b Thomson	0			
Extras	(b 1, lb 7, nb 1)		9	(b 1, lb)		4
TOTAL			166	(for 6 wkts)		132

Buss	20	4	46	1	1- 2	18.2	6	33	0	1- 6
Snow	20	6	31	1	2- 25	23	7	44	5	2- 29
Thomson	24.5	4	42	4	3- 33	13	2	24	0	3- 31
Oakman	19	9	34	3	4- 68	15	4	27	1	4- 36
Suttle	7	5	4	1	5-119	1	1	0	0	5- 70
					6-157					6-121
					7-162					
					8-165					
					9-166					
					10-166					

Worcestershire won by 4 wickets

Umpires : J.F.Crapp and P.A.Gibb

Worcestershire *v.* Sussex scorecard, 1965. Worcestershire won with just seven minutes of the extra half hour remaining, to record their seventh consecutive win. The Championship was won by four points from runners-up Northamptonshire, winning thirteen matches, drawing ten and losing four.

Dressing room celebrations at Hove. From left to right: Martin Horton, Jack Flavell, Norman Gifford, Len Coldwell, Don Kenyon, Doug Slade, Alan Ormrod, Tom Graveney (at the rear), Ron Headley, Roy Booth, Dick Richardson and Basil D'Oliveira. 1965 was the first season that D'Oliveira appeared in the County Championship after qualifying for a season with Kidderminster in the Birmingham League.

Twelve of the Worcestershire cricketers who retained the Championship title. From left to right, standing: Doug Slade (20 apps), R. Booth (25), Ron Headley (28), Basil D'Oliveira (28), Len Coldwell (18), Jim Standen (1), Norman Gifford (24). Seated: Martin Horton (21), Jack Flavell (28), Don Kenyon (19), Tom Graveney (27), Dick Richardson (27). Flavell played in every Championship match, taking 132 wickets with 10 five-wickets-in-an-innings performances, turning four of them into ten in a match.

Don Kenyon receives congratulations from former Worcestershire all-rounder Dick Howorth who was a member of the committee during this period of success. At Bournemouth in late August, Kenyon and Ingleby-Mackenzie caused controversy when the home captain declared 146 runs behind and Kenyon then declaring the second innings at 0-0 after one ball. Hampshire were left with 147 runs to win but met some remarkable bowling by Jack Flavell (5-9) and Len Coldwell (5-22) and were all out for 31 in 16.3 overs.

Brian Brain took 44 wickets at 21.34 in the 1965 Championship side with a best performance of 6-58 in a drawn match with Warwickshire at New Road. Worcester-born Brain made his debut in 1959 and took 508 wickets for Worcestershire before he was released at the end of the 1975 season. He then spent six seasons with Gloucestershire before retiring in 1981. His career best for Worcestershire was 8-55 at New Road against Essex in the second innings (having taken 3-52 in the first) during his last season with Worcestershire. As a young cricketer he showed batting promise but it never developed and his highest score for Worcestershire was modest 38 in 1964 against Gloucestershire at Cheltenham. However, his partnership of 55 for the eighth wicket with Norman Gifford – after Don Kenyon and Martin Horton had both had ducks and Worcestershire were 73-7 – was most important in helping the first innings total up to 143 and eventual victory by 107 runs.

Derek Richardson (who always answered to 'Dick') followed his brother into the Worcestershire side, playing alongside him on his debut against Oxford University in 1952. He became a regular in 1955, the season he scored his maiden century (126) at New Road against Gloucestershire, sharing a partnership of 116 for the fifth wicket with 'Laddie' Outschoorn. The best of his 16 hundreds was 169 at Dudley against Derbyshire, where he hit 27 fours. This was his fourth hundred of the season and shortly after he was selected for the Third Test against the West Indies at Trent Bridge, where he joined brother Peter for his only Test appearance. He was bowled by Garry Sobers for 33 in his only innings in a match that was a personal success for a future team-mate, Tom Graveney, who scored 258 (his career best). When he retired at the end of the 1967 season, Derek had scored 15,843 runs at 27.45 and held a Worcestershire record 416 catches, including 65 in 1961, another club record. Brother Peter left at the end of the 1958 before they had shared a century partnership together and his best for Worcestershire was with Bob Broadbent against Oxford University in 1962 when they added 222 for the fourth wicket in just over two and a half hours.

Alan Ormrod was well into his seventh season with Worcestershire before he scored his first century in 1968 against Hampshire at Portsmouth. During this innings he was at the wicket five and a half hours, hitting 11 fours, before he had to retire hurt on 123 in a Worcestershire total of 257-6 declared. Worcestershire then bowled Hampshire out for 83, Basil D'Oliveira taking 6-29 and Norman Gifford 3-18 for an 115 runs win. Ormrod made 465 first-class appearances for Worcestershire, scoring 21,753 runs with 31 hundreds – the best of them being 205 not out at Dartford against Kent in 1973 after batting seven hours and ten minutes and hitting 27 fours. He bowled occasional off-spin, having one five-wicket performance (5-27 at Bristol in 1972) and took 25 wickets in all. In the winter of 1966/67 he went to Pakistan with an MCC under-25 eleven and scored one half-century in an innings of 61 not out at Peshawar against Northern Zone. On leaving Worcestershire he joined Lancashire in 1984, playing 27 matches over two seasons before becoming their cricket manager from 1986 until 1991, a position he also held at Trent Bridge until the end of the 1998 season.

The next silverware in the cabinet at New Road was the John Player Sunday League Trophy, which Worcestershire won in 1971. From left to right, standing: Arthur Ross-Slater (scorer), Jim Yardley (14 apps), G.R. Cass (5), Vanburn Holder (16), Bob Carter (15), Alan Ormrod (16), Glenn Turner (11), Kevin Griffith (12). Seated: Basil D'Oliveira (11), Ron Headley (16), Norman Gifford (captain) (9), Doug Slade (9). Gordon Wilcock took over the wicketkeeping duties for the last twelve matches and Keith Wilkinson also played made important contributions at the end. Ted Hemsley missed the beginning and the end of the season because of soccer commitments, but had a career best 4-42 match-winning performance at New Road against Essex in July.

Ron Headley led the Worcestershire side for the last three matches after Norman Gifford broke a thumb in the Second Test at Old Trafford and was out for the rest of the season. His tenure began at New Road against Somerset, in front of BBC cameras (as all three of them were), where Worcestershire won by the narrow margin of 8 runs. In the next match rain held up play when they met the League leaders and favourites Lancashire at Old Trafford and a ten-overs-a-side affair began at ten past five. Headley won the toss and made the unheard decision to bat first. He led from the front, hitting 36 of Worcestershire's 77-3 total and then followed with some inspired field placings to restrict the home side to 67-7 and a 10 runs defeat. All now hinged on victory over Warwickshire at Dudley, where they had to improve on their run-rate to overtake Essex. Warwickshire were dismissed for 126 and in order to go top Worcestershire had to reach this target in 17.5 overs. Again Headley led from the front, top scoring with 58, and Keith Wilkinson hit the winning run with two balls to spare. Glamorgan did Worcestershire proud when they beat Lancashire at Old Trafford, on the day after Clive Lloyd's marriage to Waveney, to give Worcestershire the title.

Norman Gifford took over the captaincy from Tom Graveney for the 1971 season and, because of that thumb injury, missed seven Sunday League games but played a very important part when Hampshire were the visitors to New Road. Once more the cameras were in attendance when, with 49 runs required off 24 balls, Gifford struck a Bob Cottam over for 16 runs (including a couple of sixes) but was shortly afterwards bowled by Trevor Jesty for 20. Jim Yardley and Gordon Wilcock secured victory together off the penultimate ball.

Glenn Turner scored 308 runs in eleven innings during the 1971 season but by the time he left Worcestershire in 1982 he had become a formidable Sunday League cricketer. He was the first batsman in the competition to reach 5,000 runs and 6,000 runs and was leading run scorer until overtaken by Denis Amiss in 1985. The best of his four centuries was 147 at Horsham in 1980 where he finished on the losing side to Sussex.

Vanburn Holder and Glenn Turner were the first of the 1960s new wave of overseas cricketers to join Worcestershire and were both model professionals on and off the field. Holder was an integral part of the 1971 John Player League winning side, taking 32 wickets (still the most wickets taken in a season by a Worcestershire bowler in the competition), including two four-wickets-in-an-innings performances. The first was 4-17 at Gloucester where Worcestershire won comfortably by nine wickets and the second was 4-28 in the epic win at Old Trafford in a ten overs match. His best figures in the League were 6-33 at Lord's against Middlesex in 1972 and in June 1974 he became the first Worcestershire bowler to aggregate 100 wickets in the competition. In first-class cricket for Worcestershire he took 586 wickets at 23.08, with the best of his 28 five-wicket performances being 7-40 against Glamorgan at Cardiff in 1974, and scored one half-century. At Dudley in 1970 he hit 52 in fifty minutes (with a six out of the ground and 8 fours) against Gloucestershire, sharing a last wicket partnership of 51 with Bob Carter.

Jim Yardley, a Chaddesley Corbett born left-hander, made his debut for Worcestershire in 1967 and scored the first of his four first-class centuries against the Indians at New Road in 1971 on the day that Imran Khan and John Parker also made their Worcestershire debuts. Yardley batted for just under three hours and shared a third-wicket partnership of 139 with Alan Ormrod in a run chase that failed by 36 runs when stumps were drawn with five wickets remaining. He made his Sunday League debut in 1969 at Headingley and was one of Richard Hutton's 7-15, being given out leg-before before he had scored (one of four ducks in a Worcestershire innings of 86 all out). At the end of the 1975 season he left, with 1,090 Sunday League runs to his name, and joined Northamptonshire, for whom he scored 1,141 – thus becoming only the fourth batsman behind Roy Virgin, Roger Knight and Younis Ahmed to complete 1,000 runs for two different counties in the competition. His career best in the League was 64 against Derbyshire during his last season at New Road, including a six off Phil Russell (one of two he hit in the League – the other was also in 1975 at Chelmsford off Ray East).

The next honour for the County was the winning of the 1974 County Championship under the leadership of Norman Gifford. From left to right, standing: Gordon Wilcock (13 apps), Jim Yardley (19), John Parker (15), Brian Brain (20), John Inchmore (13), Vanburn Holder (19), Rodney Cass (6), Keith Wilkinson (3), Ian Johnson (2), Arthur Ross-Slater (scorer). Seated: Alan Ormrod (20), Basil D'Oliveira (17), Norman Gifford (20), Ron Headley (18), Glenn Turner (18). Eleven matches were won, three lost and six drawn, the last of these at Chelmsford when rain washed out play at the start of the match. At the close on Saturday (the first day) Essex were 84 all out and Worcestershire had collected four bowling points, thanks to Gifford's 7-15, to lead second-placed Hampshire by two points. Hampshire were due to play Yorkshire but rain prevented a ball being bowled so Worcestershire took their third County Championship title.

Norman Gifford took 66 wickets in the Championship in 1974 and was one of six survivors of the 1965 winners, the others being Brain, D'Oliveira, Headley, Hemsley and Ormrod. Holder took 87 wickets and Brain 75 with the leading run scorers being Turner (1,098) and Headley (1,108). Norman continued with the captaincy until handing over to Glenn Turner for the 1981 season. After one season Philip Neale took over and the next page shows Turner and Gifford receiving momentos on behalf of the club to mark their splendid service to the county at the end of the 1982 season. Turner scored 22,298 runs with 72 centuries for Worcestershire (two more than Don Kenyon) and hit his 100th hundred against Warwickshire at New Road on 29 June 1982 in a massive 311 not out (with 2 sixes and 39 fours) – which was the first triple-hundred scored in a day since Jack Robertson, on the same ground, hit 331 not out for Middlesex in 1949.

Turner, Gifford and (looking on) Mike Jones, Alec Burnett (chairman) and Jack Roberts (president). The man looking out of the dressing-room window is Hartley Alleyne.

Twelve seasons of underachieving followed until the Sunday League was won for the second time in 1987. Ian Botham and Graham Dillley had joined in the winter and several of the younger players were performing well. The side, led by Phil Neale, is seen here with the Refuge League Trophy. From left to right, standing: Stuart Lampitt (6 appearances), Martin Weston (11), Ian Botham (11), Graham Dilley (6), Steve McEwan (3), Richard Illingworth (12), Steve Rhodes (16), Gordon Lord (1). Seated: Graeme Hick (16), Neal Radford (16), Tim Curtis (16), Phil Neale (16), Paul Pridgeon (14), Damian D'Oliveira (16), Phil Newport (16). The League was won on the last Sunday of the season when they beat Northamptonshire in front of BBC cameras by nine wickets, their eleventh win of the season. Curtis (617 runs), Hick (599) and Botham (578) were the backbone of the batting and Radford took 25 wickets. The only other bowler to take 25 wickets in the League that season was Gloucestershire's Courtney Walsh.

Paul Pridgeon made his Worcestershire debut in 1972 and took 167 wickets in 161 Sunday League appearances, including 6-26 at New Road against Surrey in 1978 (still the best figures by a Worcestershire bowler in the competition). During his eighteen season first-class career he took 530 wickets with a career best 7-35 against Oxford University in 1976. His best County Championship figures were 7-44 at Grace Road in 1987 in a rain-affected drawn game against Leicestershire. Never one to stay long at the crease with the bat he hit just one fifty in the course of a 240 match career – going in as night-watchman at New Road against Warwickshire in 1984 he hit 67 in 191 minutes, facing 172 balls and sharing a third-wicket partnership of 107 with Tim Curtis. Pridgeon was a popular member of the staff as proved by his benefit cheque in 1989 of £154,720. He left at the end of that season to join the staff of Shrewsbury School.

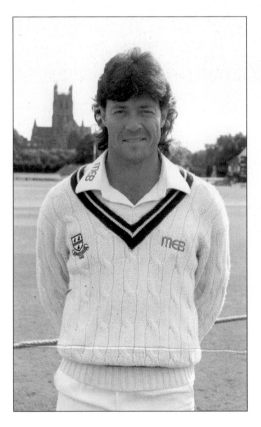

Neal Radford joined Worcestershire from Lancashire in 1985 and immediately made an impact by taking 101 first-class wickets that season, becoming the first Worcestershire bowler to take 100 wickets in a season for fifteen seasons (Norman Gifford took 105 in 1970). He repeated this performance in 1986 when he took 109 wickets and when he retired at the end of the 1995 season had taken 653 wickets for the County at 27.18 with a career best 9-70 (11-129 in the match) at New Road against Somerset in a two-days innings win in 1986. Having taken the first eight wickets to fall, including a spell of 4-1 in twelve balls, he was in sight of becoming the first bowler for twenty-two years to take all ten in an innings in England when Phil Newport broke the sequence. That season Radford made the first of his three Test appearances for England when he was selected for the Third Test against India at Edgbaston and during the winter of 1987/88 he went to New Zealand with the England touring party. He was just six wickets short of 1,000 wickets in all first-class matches over a 296 match career.

Double-winners Worcestershire seen here with the Refuge Sunday League Trophy, for the second consecutive season, in 1988. They won the competition by beating Warwickshire by ten wickets at New Road on 28 August. Nineteen days later they won their fourth County Championship title when, despite attempts made by vandals to sabotage the pitch, they beat Glamorgan by an innings and 76 runs. The players pictured are, from left to right, standing: David Leatherdale, Neal Radford, Richard Illingworth, Martin Weston, Steve O'Shaughnessy, Steve McEwan, Paul Bent, Damian D'Oliveira. Seated: Graham Dilley, Graeme Hick, Tim Curtis, Phil Neale (captain), Paul Pridgeon, Steve Rhodes, Phil Newport. The title was won again the following season with an almost identical staff to equal the exploits of Don Kenyon's 1964 and 1965 successes.

Gordon Lord joined Worcestershire from local neighbours Warwickshire in 1987, coming to the side with a career best of 199 run out against Yorkshire in 1986. In the last away match of the 1988 season Gordon Lord scored 101 out of a Worcestershire total of 199 at Bristol – last out and batting for over five hours he gave the bowlers something to bowl at, leaving Gloucestershire needing 342 runs to win. Richard Illingworth (5-63) and Graeme Hick (4-114) went on to bowl Worcestershire to an important 114 runs victory. This was Lord's maiden century for Worcestershire and he added three more with a best of 190 against Hampshire at New Road in 1990 (2 sixes and 29 fours in five-and-a-half hours, sharing an opening partnership of 167 with Curtis and a second-wicket stand of 164 with Hick). Lord left Worcestershire at the end of the 1991 season and is currently on the ECB coaching staff covering the West of England.

Graham Dilley came to Worcestershire in 1987 having had a long career with Kent and England which had begun in 1977. Most of the time he was with Worcestershire he suffered knee problems, but on several occasions had match-winning performances that helped win two County Championship titles. The best of his 13 five-wicket performances (over 52 matches) was 6-43 at New Road against Leicestershire in 1987. In all first-class matches Dilley took 171 wickets for Worcestershire at 23.05 each.

The New Road scoreboard at the close of play where the West Indians were the visitors. Graeme Hick went in to this match needing 153 runs to be only the second Worcestershire batsman (Glenn Turner was the first) to score 1,000 first-class runs before the end of May. Only W.G. Grace and Don Bradman reached this milestone in fewer innings and only Bradman was younger. To reach this 1,000 runs Hick had faced 1,345 balls, hitting 118 fours and 21 sixes. His parents had arrived from Zimbabwe just in time to see the conclusion of this monumental innings.

Graeme Hick joined Worcestershire in 1984, aged eighteen, and had an impressive debut at The Oval during Worcestershire's last match of the season, batting at number eight and scoring 82 not out during an unbroken eighth-wicket partnership of 137 with his captain, Phil Neale. Most of this season was spent with the second eleven for whom he scored 964 runs in sixteen innings at 64.26 with four centuries, the best of which was 186 at Grace Road (2 sixes and 34 fours off 252 balls in 272 minutes). He also had a successful season in the Birmingham League with Kidderminster, scoring 1,234 runs including 182 not out against Moseley. Until he had served his England qualification period in 1991, Hick was Worcestershire's overseas cricketer following the departure of Kapil Dev and Collis King in 1985. In 1986 he became the youngest batsman to aggregate 2,000 runs in a season at the age of 20 years and 111 days (beating Len Hutton by over nine months). The same season also saw him become the youngest Worcestershire batsman (aged 20 years and 46 days) to score a double-century when he scored 227 not out off a Nottinghamshire attack that contained Richard Hadlee, Clive Rice and Eddie Hemmings at New Road. Hick followed this innings with 219 not out and 52 at Neath against Glamorgan in the next match.

...TCH BETWEEN   SOMERSET AND WORCESTERSHIRE .   BRITANNIC ASSURANCE CHAMPIONSHIP

...AYED AT   TAUNTON   ON THUR, FRI, SAT, MON, MAY 5, 6, 7, 9TH

...PIRES   R. JULIAN / R. PALMER   SIDE WINNING TOSS   WORCESTERSHIRE

...RERS   D. A. OSLAM / J. W. SEWTER   1ST INNINGS OF WORCESTERSHIRE

Time for 50 150 100 200	Time IN	Time OUT	BATSMEN	RUNS AS SCORED	HOW OUT	BOWLER	
	11-0	2-09	T. S. CURTIS	①④1④1④2M12I2111	BOWLED	ROSE	2
..				144M 119B 2/-			
	11-0	2-49	G. R. LORD	314④124114322431441	CT MALLENDER	DREDGE	4
				109M 88B 4/-			
	11-50		G. A. HICK	4144224344111121214341211412222131134114224111141411694122141241121412221414	NOT	OUT	4
				552M 469B 35/11			
	2-05	2-07	D. B. D'OLIVEIRA	G.A. HICK	CT ROEBUCK	ROSE	0
				2M 2B			
	2-08	2-26	T. A. NEALE		CT MARKS	MALLENDER	0
				18M 16B			
	2-27	2-40	I. T. BOTHAM	1231/	BOWLED	ROSE	
				13M 13B			
HH 110	2-41	12-37	S. J. RHODES	2111211122711112421311241111211111111112/	CT FELTON	DREDGE	5
				311M 274B 2/-			
	12-38	2-21	P. J. NEWPORT	3313131321114	BOWLED	MARKS	2
				63M 65B 1/-			
	2-22		R. K. ILLINGWORTH	3222121211311211311	NOT	OUT	3
				106M 94B			
			N. V. RADFORD				
			G. R. DILLEY	DID NOT BAT			

B 141

L 1111111141111

NB 1111

	1 30-1	2 39-2	3 39-4	4 44-2	5 47-4	6 138-1	7 151-5	8	9	10	TOTAL	628
WICKETS	78	912	112	119	132	397	451				For	
N OUT	LORD	CURTIS	D'OLIVERA	NEALE	BOTHAM	RHODES	NEWPORT				DEC	
	CURTIS 25	HICK 32	HICK 33	HICK 39	HICK 45	HICK 242	HICK 268					

Graeme Hick's 405 not out scorecard. Graeme hit 11 sixes and 35 fours off 469 balls in 555 minutes and his 405 not out was 19 runs short of A.C. MacLaren's highest score made in England for Lancashire, also at Taunton against Somerset, in 1895. In this innings he shared Worcestershire's record partnerships for the sixth wicket (265 with Steve Rhodes in 274 balls) and for the eighth (177 with Richard Illingworth). The latter record has since been broken by Rhodes and Stuart Lampitt with 184 at Kidderminster against Derbyshire in 1991. Hick's magnificent innings was scored off what could be termed 'proper bowling' and a result was achieved in the match – slightly different circumstances to the 501 not out by Brian Lara at a later date – and he contributed 3-33 to the bowling attack.

The Britannic Assurance cheque arrives to crown the County Champions of 1988 following Worcestershire's fine innings and 76 runs win over Glamorgan at New Road shortly after lunch on 17 September.

Richard Illingworth made his first-class debut for Worcestershire in 1982 at New Road against Somerset and took his first wicket when he had Peter Roebuck caught behind by David Humphries, finishing with the creditable figures of 3-61 off 27 overs. At the end of the 1999 season he had taken 729 wickets for Worcestershire, made nine Test Match appearances and followed in the footsteps of Ted Arnold and Dick Howorth by taking a wicket with the first ball that he bowled in Test cricket (bowling Phil Simmons at Trent Bridge in the First Test against the West Indies in 1991). Two of his three Worcestershire centuries were scored against Warwickshire and both of them from coming in as a night-watchman: the first was at New Road in 1987 and the second at Edgbaston ten years later. Illingworth is the leading Worcestershire wicket-taker in the Sunday League, having taken 250 up to the end of the 1999 season, including the county's only hat-trick in any one-day competition – he bowled Peter Moores and Tony Pigott and had Ed Giddins leg-before at Hove in 1993 with the last three balls of the Sussex innings.

Steven Rhodes trod the same path as Syd Buller and Roy Booth to New Road, having made appearances for Yorkshire when he joined Worcestershire in 1985. Since that first appearance he has hardly missed a match in any of the competitions and is the only wicketkeeper to have taken 1,000 first class dismissals and 300 in the League. He has taken six dismissals in an innings twice, the first of them at Kidderminster in 1988 during the Sussex second innings, having held three in their first innings. This nine in the match equalled the Worcestershire best of Hugo Yarnold (five caught and four stumped) against Hampshire in 1949. Rhodes scored the first of his nine Worcestershire centuries in 1988 at Derby. He was 97 not out overnight and Phil Neale jokingly said that he was going to declare with the score on 332-6 on the Monday morning, but that was not to be. Rhodes had shared a 206 run partnership with Neale for the sixth wicket and went on to reach 108 in 154 minutes off 192 balls with a six and 7 fours. England recognition came first in the Texaco Trophy against the 1989 Australians and followed with Test selection in 1994 against New Zealand and South Africa followed by a visit to Australia in the Winter of 1994/95, making a total of eleven Test appearances .

Celebrations outside Buckingham Palace after Worcestershire's visit to meet the Duke of Edinburgh in the Autumn of 1988 in recognition of their County Championship success. They made this trip again the following year.

Ian Botham moved to Worcestershire for the start of the 1987 season following the turmoil over the sackings of Viv Richards and Joel Garner by Somerset. He made a modest debut at New Road against Kent, hitting 46 and 25 and taking 2-125 in the match. On his return to Taunton in July he scored his maiden century for Worcestershire with 126 not out from 111 balls, but rain ended the match with the Worcestershire total on 337-4 and it was abandoned as a draw. At the beginning of August during this first season he began to open with Tim Curtis in the Refuge League: they had a record four consecutive century partnerships that helped Worcestershire to four wins and the League title. They began 1998 in this competition opening together but it soon came to an end when Botham had to have a major back operation that put him out for the rest of the season, although his enthusiasm provided morale-boosting encouragement in the dressing-room towards the Championship and League double. He stayed with Worcestershire until the end of the 1991 season and then joined first-class newcomers Durham having scored 2,097 runs at 30.39 with four centuries and taken 131 wickets at 25.74 with a best of 7-54 against Warwickshire at New Road during his last season.

Tim Curtis was born in Kent but raised in
Worcester, where he was educated at the
Royal Grammar School, and arrived at New
Road having come through the
Worcestershire Cricket Association schools
system. He is mentioned in the first edition of
the WCA *Year Book 1976* in the under-16s
section: 'T. Curtis (Barnard's Green)
dominated the innings making a fine 52, to
enable us to gain a comfortable 6 wicket
victory'. He was nineteen when he made his
debut against Sri Lanka in 1979 and by the
time he retired at the end of 1997 had scored
20,155 runs with 43 centuries, including at
least one against every other county. Two of
these were turned into doubles, the best of
them being 248 against Somerset at New
Road in 1991, adding 256 for the third wicket
with David Leatherdale. Curtis captained the
county from 1992 until he handed over to
Tom Moody during the 1995 season and
appeared in five Test Matches between 1988
and 1989. During the winter breaks he taught
at his old school and is now installed there
full-time – one of his pupils is a certain
Daniel Jackson, grandson of Don Kenyon.

Martin Weston also made his debut in the
above-mentioned tourist match in 1979,
scoring 43 in his only appearance of the season.
Between that first appearance and the start of
the 1982 season Weston had made only seven
appearances, but after an innings of 63 against
Zimbabwe he had more opportunities and
impressed with 93 against the Pakistanis. He
scored the first of his three centuries in 1983
against Sussex at Hove, adding 171 for the
third wicket with Dipak Patel. This innings of
115 was mentioned in *Wisden*, who described
him as a 'solid young opener'. In 1982 at
Taunton he scored his only Sunday League
hundred when he hit 109 against Somerset in
an innings containing 5 sixes (three off Colin
Dredge and two off Hallam Moseley) and
7 fours; this was the only century in the
competition by a Worcester-born cricketer.
Weston was capped in 1986 and shared a
benefit with Damian D'Oliveira in 1993,
retiring at the end of the season with 5,597
runs at 23.91 and 82 wickets at 39.07, followed
by 16 Minor Counties appearances for
Herefordshire between 1994 and 1996.

Ian Botham acknowledges the crowd after the 131 runs win over Gloucestershire at New Road This victory secured Worcestershire's second County Championship title in succession with a game in hand, although this was helped by the 25 point penalty suffered by Essex for a substandard pitch at Southend.

More celebrations on the balcony where Phil Neale is calling the season's performance 'a greater achievement than last year, because of all our injuries and Test calls. I am proud of the squad, particularly the youngsters who have done so well for us'.

Even after five County Championship and three Sunday League titles, winning at Lord's in a one-day final seemed an impossibility. Ted Dexter and Don Kenyon, pictured here on the dressing room balcony, were the first captains in a one-day final at Lord's when Sussex beat Worcestershire by 14 runs in the dark. Nornan Gifford, with 4-33 in the Sussex total of 168, was the first Man of the Match and the first six in a Lord's final was struck by Jim Parks (over extra cover, off Doug Slade). The matches were of 65 overs-a-side for the first year, reduced to 60 in 1964 and further reduced to 50 for 1999 – thus robbing supporters of 30 overs of cricket since that inaugural season. Kenyon took Worcestershire to the 1966 final when they were beaten by Warwickshire and Gifford took them in the Benson & Hedges Cup final in 1973 and 1976 when they were beaten each time by Kent. The menu below was meant for a celebration after the 1988 NatWest final, but a fine 56 by Man of the Match Mark Ramprakash, after Mike Gatting had been run out without facing, saw Middlesex home by three wickets. Once again in 1990 a Lord's final ended in disappointment when Lancashire won by 69 runs in the Benson & Hedges Cup. However, success was just around the corner.

REGENTS PARK LOUNGE
CRICKET SPECIAL

ON THE OCCASION OF

THE

NATWEST BANK TROPHY FINAL

MIDDLESEX V WORCESTERSHIRE

SATURDAY 3rd SEPTEMBER 1988

AT LORDS

MENU

SELECTION OF SANDWICHES	£2.95
SOUP OF THE DAY	£2.95
OGEN MELON & ORANGE COCKTAIL	£3.25

******

HOME-MADE LASAGNE	£7.95
SIRLOIN STEAK	£9.75
FRIED SCAMPI & TARTARE SAUCE	£9.50

******

FRESH FRUIT SALAD	£2.95
STRAWBERRY CHEESECAKE	£2.95
APPLE STRUDEL	£2.95

******

| FRESHLY BREWED COFFEE | £1.25 |

At last! Phil Neale takes the catch at cover off Graham Dilley to end Lancashire's effort when last man Paul Allott goes leaving Worcestershire winners by 65 runs.

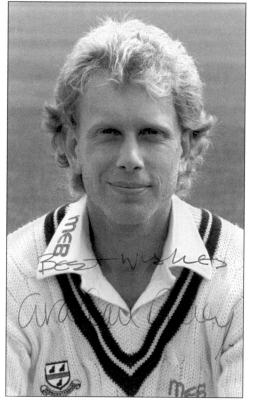

Light rain was falling on that Saturday morning but for once the weather was not the main talking point. When the Lancashire side was announced it was without its captain, David Hughes, who stood down after discussions with his players, leaving Neil Fairbrother to take over. Play began late and Fairbrother's first mistake was not to put pressure on Graeme Hick, who came in following the early dismissal of Tim Curtis. Hick struck his first ball for four off Paul Allott, and made another nine fours before he was brilliantly caught and bowled by Allott for 88. Richard Illingworth and Neal Radford added 33 priceless runs (off 22 balls) for the ninth wicket, with Wasim Akram going for 18 runs off his last over. Lancashire's reply was interrupted by rain with the score at 32-3 after Gehan Mendis, Mike Atherton and Neil Fairbrother had already been sent back to the pavilion. Play resumed on the Sunday in bright sunshine and Worcestershire gradually worked their way through the Lancashire batting with Graham Hick taking three catches at second slip – one of them off Graham Dilley, whose mean figures and that dramatic last catch by Neale helped Worcestershire to their first one-day knock-out trophy.

```
                        BENSON and HEDGES CUP FINAL  1991

        Lancashire  v Worcestershire  at Lord's  Saturday and Sunday 13 and 14 July

        Toss won by : Lancashire who chose to field

        Man of the match : Graeme Hick

        Worcestershire

        T.S.Curtis                        b DeFreitas    4
        T.M.Moody                         b Allott      12
        G.A.Hick                   c & b Allott         88
        D.B.D'Oliveira c DeFreitas b Wasim Akram        25
        I.T.Botham     c Fowler    b Watkinson          19
        *P.A.Neale     c Watkinson b Austin             4
        +S.J.Rhodes    c Allott    b Wasim Akram        13
        R.K.Illingworth    not        out              17
        P.J.Newport    c DeFreitas b Wasim Akram        2
        N.V.Radford        not        out              25
        G.R.Dilley     did not bat
            Extras     (b 0, 1b 8, w 15, nb 4)          27
                                                       ---
            TOTAL          (for 8 wkts)                236

        DeFreitas      11   1   38   1      1-  4
        Allott         11   3   26   2      2- 38
        Watkinson      11   0   54   1      3- 97
        Wasim Akram    11   1   58   3      4-166
        Austin         11   0   52   1      5-172
                                            6-175
                                            7-195
                                            8-203


        Lancashire            1st Innings

        G.D.Mendis                        b Radford     14
        G.Fowler       c Hick      b Radford            54
        M.A.Atherton   c Rhodes    b Radford            5
        *N.H.Fairbrother   run out                      1
        G.D.lloyd      c Hick      b Botham             10
        M.Watkinson    c Hick      b Dilley             13
        Wasim Akram        run out                      14
        P.A.J.DeFreitas c Neale   b Newport            19
        +W.K.Hegg          not        out              13
        I.D.Austin     c Illingworth b Newport          7
        P.J.W.Allott   c Neale     b Dilley            10
            Extras     (b 0, 1b 5, w 4, nb 2)          11
                                                       ---
            TOTAL                                      171

        Dilley         8.2  2   19   2      1- 24
        Radford        9    1   48   3      2- 31
        Botham         8    1   23   1      3- 32
        Newport        11   1   38   2      4- 64
        Illingworth    11   0   38   0      5- 92
                                            6-111
                                            7-134
                                            8-140
                                            9-158
                                           10-171

                            Worcestershire won by 65 runs

                      Umpires : J.W.Holder and D.R.Shepherd
```

Worcestershire *v.* Lancashire, 1991
Benson & Hedges final.

MARYLEBONE CRICKET CLUB

BENSON & HEDGES - CUP FINAL

at LORD'S, SATURDAY 13th JULY, 1991

Admit ..... Don Kenyon .....

TO BOX ..P/Q.. IN THE TAVERN STAND

THIS PASS DOES NOT ADMIT TO THE GROUND

Phil Neale holds the Benson & Hedges trophy aloft on the Lord's balcony: this was Worcestershire's lucky seventh attempt at a winning a Lord's final.

Graham Hick proudly acknowledges the crowd after receiving the Man of the Match award in the Benson & Hedges Cup final. Hick was on the scene early after Tim Curtis played on to the last ball of the first over and stayed to face 126 balls, hitting 10 fours in his innings of 88. He followed this with three catches taken at second slip.

The Worcestershire squad sporting the Benson & Hedges Cup and the Refuge Cup at the start of the 1992 season. The latter trophy was won later in the 1991 season at Old Trafford when Worcestershire inflicted yet another defeat on Lancashire, this time by a closer margin of 7 runs. Steve Rhodes, deputising for Tom Moody who had joined the Australians for a Zimbabwe tour, opened with Tim Curtis and scored 105, the first and last century in the 12 match, four-year-old competition. This was Rhodes' first one-day hundred, coming off 127 balls, and it won him the Man of the Match award. From left to right, standing: Kevin Lyons (coach), Stuart Bevins, David Leatherdale, Richard Stemp, James Brinkley, Philip Weston, Adam Seymour, Alex Wylie, Chris Tolley, Gavin Haynes, Matt Dallaway, Mark Scott (assistant coach). Seated: Stuart Lampitt, Graham Dilley, Phil Newport, Neal Radford, Phil Neale, Tim Curtis, Damian D'Oliveira, Graeme Hick, Richard Illingworth, Martin Weston, Tom Moody. Steven Rhodes had not returned from the England A tour of Bermuda and the West Indies when this photograph was taken.

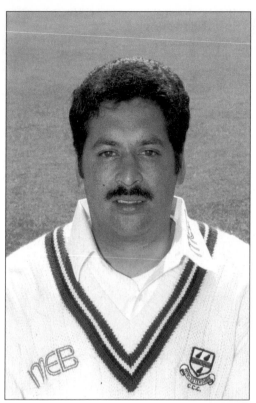

During the 1991 Benson & Hedges triumph, Damian D'Oliveira had brilliantly ran out the Lancashire captain, Neil Fairbrother, second ball, with a direct hit from mid-wicket at the non-striker's end, leaving them floundering on 32-3. D'Oliveira joined Worcestershire in 1978, making one Second XI Championship appearance that year, and in the following season appeared once with his father, Basil – who was then coach – against Northamptonshire Seconds at New Road. He spent two years with the MCC Young Professionals at Lord's and made his first-class debut for Worcestershire in 1982 against Zimbabwe at New Road, finally becoming a regular in 1983. During the 1989 Championship season he scored 766 runs at 21.27. After his last match in 1995 he had scored 9,476 runs at 27.70, including ten centuries. The best of these, 237, came in the Parks against Oxford University in 1991 from 219 balls in 217 minutes, with 7 sixes and 31 fours, adding 243 for the fifth wicket with David Leatherdale. On his retirement he joined the Worcestershire coaching staff and is currently assistant to Bill Athey.

Phil Neale took over the captaincy from Glenn Turner in 1982 and a steady improvement took place under his leadership, eventually bringing two County Championship successes, two Sunday League titles and the first ever one-day knock-out win at Lord's. He made his debut in 1975 and the following season, his first as a regular, he finished just 51 short of 1,000 runs – not an unusual situation for Philip. Including that season, he ended seven seasons in the 900s, whilst he actually got to 1,000 on seven occasions. Capped in 1978 and awarded a benefit in 1988, he became the first Worcestershire cricketer to receive a six-figure cheque (for £153,005). By the time he left at the end of the 1992 season he had scored 17,431 runs at 36.46, a fine average for someone who was never selected for England, and had hit 28 centuries. The best of these was 167 against Sussex at Kidderminster in 1988, 102 of his runs coming in boundaries with a six and 24 fours. He took over the post of director of cricket at Northampton in 1993, during which time he managed England A in South Africa during the winter of 1993/1994 and India in 1994/1995. Currently he is manager of England on their 1999/2000 tours of South Africa and Zimbabwe.

Further success followed in 1994 when, having lost to them in two Lord's finals (the Gillette Cup in 1966 and in the Benson & Hedges Cup that July), Worcestershire went to the NatWest final in September and beat Warwickshire by a comfortable eight-wicket margin. This was the only trophy that Warwickshire did not win in that season and it was made all the sweeter when their former overseas cricketer, Tom Moody, took the Man of the Match award. Having been put in by captain Tim Curtis, Warwickshire got 223-9 off their 60 overs, Brian Lara top scoring with 88. Tom Moody and Graeme Hick put together an unbroken third-wicket partnership of 198 off 212 balls and saw Worcestershire home with more than ten overs to spare.

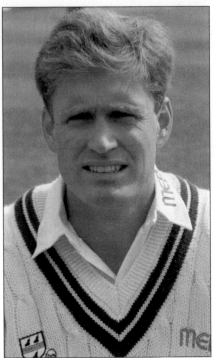

Tom Moody joined Worcestershire at the beginning of the 1991 season to replace Graeme Hick (who became qualified as an English player) as their overseas cricketer, having spent one season with Warwickshire in 1990. He made an immediate impression in his first Sunday League match when he scored 160 off 111 balls in 121 minutes (6 sixes and 16 fours), the highest innings in the competition for a county debut. By the end of the season he had scored 917 runs in the League (still a record) and had an aggregate of 1,887 first-class runs at 62.90, finishing top of the Worcestershire averages, with six centuries. Including in those six hundreds was his Worcestershire career best of 212 against Nottinghamshire at New Road in 1996, where he added 199 for the fourth wicket with Reuben Spiring. Moody took over the Worcestershire captaincy mid-way through the 1995 season, a position he has held with Western Australia since 1995/96 – leading them to the last two Sheffield Shield titles. Eight Australian Test caps have come his way and he was an integral part of the 1999 Australian World Cup winning side in England.

Phil Newport made his debut for Worcestershire in 1982 at New Road against the Pakistani tourists, but had to wait until his Championship debut at Edgbaston over a month later for his first scalp when took the prize wicket of Dennis Amiss, bowled for 57, in a high scoring drawn game. He had taken 825 wickets for Worcestershire in all first-class matches at the end of the 1999 season and had a three match Test career, taking ten wickets. In the final against Warwickshire he had an excellent return of 4-38, moving the ball around to such an extent that it took Lara 26 balls to get off the mark. Phil retired at the end of the 1999 season.

Five
Cricketing Footballers

R.E. Foster is the only man to captain England at cricket and soccer. During his time at Oxford University he made his England soccer debut against Wales in 1900 at Cardiff and the following season, as a Corinthian player, he made three more international appearances, scoring twice against Ireland at Southampton and once against Wales at St James' Park, Newcastle (where Steve Bloomer scored four goals in a 6-0 win). In the match at Southampton C.B. Fry won his only cap and Ernie Needham (Derbyshire CCC) played left half. Foster played once more, against Wales, in 1902.

G. GAUKRODGER,
WORCESTERSHIRE.

J. A. CUFFE.
WORCESTERSHIRE

Left: Fred Wheldon, a colleague of R.E. Foster in Worcestershire's first first-class match in 1899 against Yorkshire, was at the time an international inside forward with Aston Villa, for whom he made 137 appearances, scoring 74 goals. In 1897 he made his debut for England at Nottingham and impressed immediately by scoring three goals in a 6-0 win over Ireland. Alongside him that day, at centre forward, was Surrey and England cricketer G.O. Smith, who was winning one of his 19 caps. Wheldon went on to play three more times the following season, scoring three more goals. He was a member of the Aston Villa side that did the FA Cup and First Division double during the 1896/97 season, scoring 18 League goals as well as Villa's second in the 3-2 win over Everton in the Cup Final at Crystal Palace. He later played for West Bromwich Albion, Queens Park Rangers and Portsmouth and joined Worcester City in 1905 at the time he was playing for Worcestershire. During his time with Worcestershire he scored 4,938 runs with three centuries, the best of them being 112 at New Road against Somerset in 1903. His grandson, John Spilsbury, a regular centre half with Worcester City, completed a unique family double when he played for Worcestershire against the Combined Services in 1952. *Centre and right:* Two more useful soccer players who were also Worcestershire cricketers were featured in a nostalgic series of Taddy tobacco cards, reproduced by London company MCIL. George Gaukrodger, a Yorkshire-born inside forward with Linfield, somehow found himself in the Northern Ireland side against Wales at Belfast in 1895, scoring once in a 2-2 draw which represented his only international appearance. John Cuffe made 279 Football League appearances for Glossop between the 1905/06 and 1914/15 season. Glossop were then in the Second Division, having been relegated from the top flight at the end of the 1899/1900 season. The first time that Gaukrodger, Cuffe and Wheldon appeared together for Worcestershire was against the 1903 touring Philadelphians in a 215 runs win at New Road and all three shared another fifteen matches together before Wheldon retired at the end of the 1906 season. In 1909 another soccer player appeared when Harold Bache, a centre forward for West Bromwich Albion, joined Cuffe and Gaukrodger against Yorkshire. Bache made 17 appearances for Worcestershire but sadly lost his life at Ypres in the First World War.

Vic Fox, seen here in 1923 (extreme right of the front row), was a Middlesbrough full-back. He moved to Wolverhampton Wanderers in March 1925, making his debut at Molineux against Leicester City. When he left Wolves for Newport County in the winter of 1928 he had made 44 League and 5 FA Cup appearances. At New Road in 1923 he shared a (then) Worcestershire record stand of 306 for the third wicket with Leonard Crawley, but Lord Harris, the custodian of cricket's laws, found that both Fox and Crawley were not properly qualified. Fox qualified with Dudley in the Birmingham League during 1924 and 1925, and returned to Worcestershire for 1926, but Crawley moved to Essex. The photograph shows, from left to right, standing: G.E.B. Abell, C.R. Preece, C.B. Ponsonby, G.B. Sanderson, L.E. Gale. Seated: L.E. Crawley, F.A. Pearson, M.K. Foster (captain), Lord Coventry, C.F. Root, W.V. Fox. Inset: H.L. Higgins.

Worcestershire v. Warwickshire at Edgbaston in 1919. This was part of a series of two-day friendlies after the First World War when Worcestershire did not enter the County Championship. From left to right, standing: R.A. Cave-Rogers, A. Machell (scorer), F. Hunt, R.D. Burrows, A.J. Conway, E.W. Bale, H.W. Isaac. Seated: A.T. Cliff, J.A. Higgs-Walker, J.W.C. Turner (captain), W.H.N. Shakespeare, F.J. Abbott. Conway made his Worcestershire debut in 1910 and at Moreton-in-Marsh in 1914 took a career best 9-38 in the Gloucestershire first innings, following this with 6-49 in the second – his 15-87 being the best match figures by a Worcestershire bowler in first-class cricket. In a five season career, before and after the First World War, he took 53 wickets at 35.92 in 29 matches. Conway also had two seasons with Wolverhampton Wanderers, making his debut at centre half in October 1908 at Molineux against Gainsborough Trinity in Football League Division Two. After a total of 30 appearances, his Wolves career came to an end with an away match against Grimsby Town in April 1910.

George Dews had an unfortunate first-class debut for Worcestershire against Lancashire at Old Trafford in 1946. In the first innings he was caught by Jack Ikin off Eric Price in the first innings before he had scored and in the second innings a pair was recorded when he was leg-before to the same bowler, again for 0. Despite this inauspicious start, George was an important part of the Worcestershire line-up in those early years after the Second World War and it was his only club as far as cricket was concerned. His soccer career, however, had more of the traveller about it. Because of the war he was almost twenty-five years old before he made his Worcestershire debut and just a little bit older when he made his Football League debut for Middlesbrough, moving on to Plymouth Argyle in 1947 and ending his soccer career with Walsall, for whom he had one season (1955/56), scoring once at Fellows Park in front of 11,469 supporters in a 2-1 win over Gillingham. He made 299 Football League appearances with his three football clubs and 374 for Worcestershire, scoring 16,671 with twenty hundreds (the best being 145 when the Combined Services were the visitors to New Road in 1951).

Henry Horton followed his brother Joe into the Worcestershire side, but soccer caused him to move south. At the time he made his Worcestershire debut in 1946 he was playing his football with Worcester City, but a sizeable fee of £2,000 for a non-League footballer was paid by Blackburn Rovers to take him to Ewood Park. He made his debut at centre half at home against Stoke City in April 1947, but became a regular at either wing half or inside forward. In June 1951 he joined Southampton and moved to play cricket with Hampshire, making his debut for them in 1953. Horton was never a regular at New Road, playing in just eleven matches before he left at the end of the 1949 season, although he blossomed with Hampshire, finishing his career with them on 21,536 runs with 32 centuries over fifteen seasons. He also made 75 League appearances for Southampton before joining Bradford for the 1954/55 season. When he left League football he joined Hereford United in the Southern League. After leaving Hampshire he returned to Worcestershire for two spells as coach inbetween a spell on the first-class umpires list (from 1973 to 1976). Before his retirement he was groundsman at the Worcester Royal Grammar School and he died in November 1998, four days before his older brother, Joe.

Jack Flavell leads Worcestershire out for his last session at New Road in August 1967. He finished off the Lancashire innings with a perfect out-swinger to Brian Statham which was caught by Alan Ormrod at slip for a 16 runs win. The players applauding Flavell are, from left to right: Len Coldwell (behind Flavell), Norman Gifford, Ron Headley, Duncan Fearnley, Ted Hemsley, Alan Ormrod, Kevin Griffith, Bob Carter, Doug Slade and Roy Booth. Flavell, who was captaining the side in the absence of Don Kenyon, made his last appearance a week later at Colwyn Bay. His football career had begun at the Hawthorns but he never got past the Central League stage with West Bromwich Albion and joined Walsall for the 1953/54 season, making 22 League and 5 FA Cup appearances – most of these were at full-back, although he played centre forward on three occasions. However, Walsall finished bottom of the old Division Three (South) and at the end of the season Flavell left to concentrate on his very successful cricket career.

Jim Standen, on the players' balcony with Basil D'Oliveira, remembers the year 1964 very well. On 2 May he kept goal for West Ham United in a 3-2 win over Preston North End at Wembley and collected a FA Cup winner's medal, then at the end of the cricket season he was a member of the Worcestershire side that won the County Championship and was top of the national bowling averages with 64 wickets at 13.00! In May the following year Standen was part of the Hammers' European Cup Winners Cup side that beat TSV Munich 2-0 at Wembley, but he played only one game for Worcestershire in 1965 and one in 1966, although he appeared more often the following three summers, finishing his career at the end of the 1970 season. After investing in sports shops in Camberley and Chertsey in Surrey, he and his wife Elise emigrated to the United States and are now living in San Francisco, where his wife was a highly-paid vice-president of an American bank. In October 1994 he put all his sporting memorabilia up for auction at Christie's in Glasgow and one of the items was the first Man of the Match award won by a Worcestershire cricketer: Standen had received this for his 5-14 performance at New Road against Surrey in Worcestershire's first Gillette Cup match in 1963. The author is sorry to say that he made an unsuccessful postal bid of £150 – the price realised being £160.

Jim Cumbes was another footballing cricketer who held silverware from both games, although not in the same calendar year. He was a member of the Worcestershire side that won the 1974 County Championship and, the following March, was the Aston Villa goalkeeper at Wembley where Ray Graydon scored the winner in the League Cup final against Norwich City. Cumbes was a much-travelled man, playing his cricket with Lancashire, Surrey, Worcestershire and Warwickshire and his soccer with a host of clubs, beginning with Runcorn and followed by Tranmere Rovers, West Bromwich Albion, Aston Villa, Portland Timbers (USA), Coventry City, Southport, Worcester City and Kidderminster Harriers. For Worcestershire he made 109 appearances, taking 246 wickets, with a best of 6-24 against Yorkshire at New Road in 1977, including three wickets in four balls. A month earlier he had gone one better when he dismissed George Sharp, Bishan Bedi and Jim Griffiths with consecutive balls, thus finishing off the Northamptonshire innings with a hat-trick. After retiring from both games, Cumbes went into cricket administration at Edgbaston and is currently a popular chief executive at Old Trafford.

The Worcestershire side at the beginning of the 1980. From left to right, standing: Barry Jones, Phil Neale, Jim Cumbes, Paul Pridgeon, Martin Weston, Hartley Alleyne, Dipak Patel, David Humphries. Seated: John Inchmore, Glenn Turner, Norman Gifford, Alan Ormrod, Ted Hemsley, Vanburn Holder. As well as League professionals Neale, Cumbes and Hemsley together in this picture, both Pridgeon and Inchmore played soccer at a good level with Stourbridge and Oldbury United respectively and Turner's Yorkshire-born grandfather had West Bromwich Albion connections. Cumbes, Hemsley and Neale were in the same first-class side seven times in 1980, but in 1978 and 1979 they appeared 19 times together – in all the trio appeared together in 69 matches between 1975 and 1981.

Ted Hemsley, a reliable defender with Shrewsbury Town, Sheffield United and Doncaster Rovers, made his Worcestershire debut in 1963. Before leaving Shrewsbury he made 215 League appearances (scoring 21 goals) and made his debut for United during the 1968/69 season in the First Division. After 247 appearances and 8 goals he joined Billy Bremner at Doncaster Rovers and retired after two seasons. For Worcestershire he scored 9,740 runs during a twenty-season career that ended in 1982, with a career best 176 not out in 1977 against Lancashire at New Road (sharing a fourth-wicket partnership of 213 with Glenn Turner on a pitch that was reported by the umpires as being unfit for first-class cricket). He was a fine one-day cricketer and won three Man of the Match awards in the Benson & Hedges Cup, two of them against Warwickshire.

Ian Botham made a brief entry into League Football with Scunthorpe United in March 1980 when he was selected as substitute for two matches in the Fourth Divison. His debut came at Dean Court against Bournemouth in a 3-3 draw and at The Old Showground he went on against Wigan Athletic where the visitors won 3-1. The following season he began four games, wearing the number nine shirt, but failed to get on the score sheet or on the winning side in any of them and his League football career petered out.

Manders Paints Presents

CHARITY FOOTBALL MATCH
in aid of
Birmingham Children's Hospital Leukaemia Fund

GRAHAM TURNER'S WOLVES

PHIL NEALE'S
WORCESTERSHIRE XI

MOLINEUX
5th December 1989
Kick Off 7.30 p.m

£1.00   **ALL CONTRIBUTIONS GO TO CHARITY**

Worcestershire played against the might of Wolves on a sharp December evening at Molineux in aid of the Birmingham Children's Hospital Leukaemia Fund. Phil Neale was heavily involved with this fund as his son, Craig, was recovering from the illness at the time.

Phil Neale was the last of the regular footballing cricketers, having a long career with Worcestershire and making 335 appearances for Lincoln City. He was the last of the 'regular' football cricketers because Tony Cottey made two appearances for Swansea City in the 1984/85 season, coming on as substitute at Vetch Field against Bristol Rovers eighteen days after Neale had made the last of his appearances for Lincoln City (coming on as substitute at Sincil Bank against Doncaster Rovers). The seasons overlap too much now for someone to succeed at the highest level in both sports, but the author well-remembers a visit to the cricket with his father at Stourbridge in 1946 when 'Raich' Carter, that brilliant Sunderland, Derby County and England inside forward made his first-class debut for Derbyshire against Worcestershire. Legend has it that, because of the lack of clothing coupons, he wore a white England football shirt and took the wickets of Eddie Cooper and Ronnie Bird for 39 runs.

Six

Home Grounds

A view from 'under the spreading chestnut trees', showing the members' pavilion and, to the left, the Ladies' pavilion, internationally known for the quality of its teas. In this 1984 photograph, taken by the late John Featherstrone, the benches in the foreground have disappeared and have been replaced by a sponsor's marquee.

New Road from the air.

A view from the top of the Cathedral taken by Patrick Eagar in the summer of 1974.

A flooded New Road in November 1984. Roy McLaren had four such situations in the winter of 1998/99 and groundsmen before him, including Fred Hunt, George Platt, Syd Styler, Mike Biddle, Gordon Prosser and Richard Stevens, have all had to cope with the same problem.

A Christmas card setting taken by Ken Edwards on Friday 13 February 1991.

Another view from under the trees. On the extreme left is the Severn Bar, for which money was raised by the volunteers of the Supporters Association. It was opened by the then President of the club, Sir George Dowty, in 1965. Sadly that bar has since disappeared and been replaced by a shop that sells replica kit. In the centre of the picture, to the left of the scoreboard, is the supporters shop which is always manned by volunteers. The church in the centre is the All Saints' parish church and to the right is the spire that is all that is left of St Andrew's church.

Ice skating at New Road in the 1950s. This adds to the list of sports seen at the ground with athletics, tennis and bowls already being performed there, whilst in September 1984 the United States beat England in a lacrosse international.

The first visit to New Road of Lord Runcie, the Archbishop of Canterbury, on 18 May 1980 for the thirteenth centenary celebrations of the Worcester Diocese.

Freeman's Garage at Southport provided this helicopter to help dry the pitch for the NatWest semi-final against Sussex in August 1986. Sussex won this one-day match (that took three to finish) by five wickets and former Worcestershire Royal Grammar schoolboy and Worcestershire all-rounder, Imran Khan, won the Man of the Match award.

Worcestershire's first match at Stourbridge

Worcestershire v Leicestershire at Amblecote, Stourbridge

26th, 27th June 1905

Worcestershire won the toss and batted

Worcestershire　　　　1st Innings

* Mr H.K.Foster	c Whiteside	b Gill	3
F.L.Bowley		b Odell	217
F.A.Pearson	c Coe	b Gill	19
J.A.Cuffe		b Odell	25
E.G.Arnold		b King	134
Mr W.E.Hutchings	c Whiteside	b Jayes	29
G.F.Wheldon		b Jayes	0
Mr W.B.Burns		b Jayes	5
+ G.W.Gaukrodger		b Jayes	12
R.D.Burrows		b King	0
G.A.Wilson	not	out	2
Extras	(b 3, lb 5, w 3, nb 0)		11

TOTAL			457

Jayes	26	2	104	4	1- 12
Gill	24	5	80	2	2- 43
Odell	29	6	96	2	3-123
Coe	10	2	43	0	4-339
King	19.5	5	63	2	5-389
Whitehead	3	1	4	0	6-389
Wood	3	0	14	0	7-400
Crawford	5	0	42	0	8-431
					9-433
					10-457

Leicestershire　　　　1st Innings　　　　　　2nd Innings (following-on)

* Mr.C.E.de Trafford	b Arnold	5	c Foster	b Arnold	18
Mr C.J.B.Wood	b Arnold	2	c Burns	b Cuffe	0
J.H.King	b Wilson	9	c Hutchings	b Wilson	26
A.E.Knight	b Arnold	2	c Burns	b Cuffe	0
H.Whitehead c Foster	b Cuffe	39	c Pearson	b Wilson	27
Mr V.F.S.Crawford	b Arnold	32	not	out	5
S.Coe	b Wilson	0		b Arnold	24
T.Jayes	b Arnold	6	c Wheldon	b Wilson	3
Mr W.W.Odell	not out	8		b Wilson	0
G.C.Gill c Wilson	b Cuffe	24		b Arnold	0
+J.P.Whiteside c Hutchings b Cuffe		0	c Hutchings	b Arnold	0
Extras	(b 9, lb 1, w 0, nb 0)	10	(b 7, lb 3, w 0, nb 0)		10
		---			---
TOTAL		137			113

Arnold	18	2	58	5	1- 5	13	1	54	4	1- 18
Wilson	9	0	38	2	2- 8	6	1	17	4	2- 22
Cuffe	9	1	31	3	3- 18	7	1	29	2	3- 22
Pearson					4- 18	1	0	3	0	4- 65
					5- 22					5- 65
					6- 95					6- 96
					7-100					7- 97
					8-101					8-113
					9-137					9-113
					10-137					10-113

Worcestershire won by an innings and 207 runs

Umpires : S.Brown and F.W.Marlow

The scorecard from the first match at Stourbridge.

The ground at Amblecote is about a quarter of a mile outside the Stourbridge town centre towards Dudley and was opened on 24 August 1857 for a two-day match between the Earl of Stamford's XI and twenty-two of the Stourbridge Club. On the death of Stamford the ownership passed on to his niece, Lady Gray, and it is presumed that she gave the ground to the Stourbridge Council in the early 1900s. The ground was actually in the old County of Staffordshire and rent was paid to Stourbridge and rates to Amblecote (respectively in Worcestershire and Staffordshire).

The last match to be played here was in 1981 and it began on 29 July, the day of the wedding of Prince Charles and Lady Diana Spencer. Glenn Turner scored a century before lunch on the first morning and added another in the second innings, but locally-born Jim Yardley, with 65 not out, saved Northamptonshire who were eight wickets down at the end and 135 runs behind.

WORCESTERSHIRE'S FIRST MATCH AT DUDLEY

Worcestershire v Gloucestershire at Tipton Road, Dudley

28th, 29th, 30th August 1911

Toss won by Worcestershire who chose to bat.

Worcestershire	1st Innings				2nd Innings		
F.L.Bowley	c Parker	b Dennett	17	lbw		b Parker	4
F.A.Pearson		b Parker	26	c Parker		b Dennett	42
E.G.Arnold		b Parker	17		c & b Dennett		13
H.K.Foster	c Luce	b Brownlee	44	c Brownlee		b Parker	12
W.B.Burns		b Parker	6			b Jessop	37
G.N.Foster	c Bowles	b Parker	0			b Dennett	0
J.A.Cuffe	c Bowles	b Dennett	16			b Jessop	32
*G.H.T.Simpson-Hayward	run out		12			b Jessop	11
H.F.Baker	not	out	8			b Jessop	5
R.D.Burrows	c Board	b Parker	2	c Luce		b Dennett	11
+E.W.Bale	c Board	b Dennett	9	not		out	0
Extras	(b 3, lb 4, w 0, nb 0)		7	(b 4, lb 0, w 0, nb 0)			4
TOTAL			164				171

Dennett	37.5	16	54	3	1- 35	30	7	74	4	1- 10
Parker	39	11	90	5	2- 50	22	4	61	2	2- 40
Brownlee	4	2	13	1	3- 96					3- 80
Jessop					4-102	7.3	0	32	4	4- 90
					5-102					5- 90
					6-125					6-118
					7-130					7-134
					8-138					8-156
					9-150					9-160
					10-164					10-171

Gloucestershire	1st Innings				2nd Innings		
+ J.H.Board	run out		18	c Pearson		b Cuffe	6
A.E.Dipper		b Arnold	0			b Arnold	2
T.Langdon	lbw	b Cuffe	15	c Foster G.N		b Cuffe	13
F.B.Roberts	c Burrows	b Cuffe	1	c Foster G.N		b Cuffe	4
*G.L.Jessop	c Bale	b Cuffe	22	c Bale		b Cuffe	8
W.M.Brownlee		b Cuffe	62	c Burns		b Arnold	23
F.M.Luce		b Cuffe	0	st Bale		b Cuffe	6
J.J.Bowles		b Arnold	2	st Bale		b Cuffe	2
A.S.Nott	c Baker	b Cuffe	4	not		out	13
E.G.Dennett	run out		16	c Foster H.K		b Cuffe	14
C.W.L.Parker	not	out	1			b Cuffe	5
Extras	(b 2, lb 1, w 0, nb 0)		3	(b 1, lb 3, w 0, nb 0)			4
TOTAL			144				100

Cuffe	18.3	3	74	6	1- 0	17.5	3	41	8	1- 6
Arnold	15	3	58	2	2- 30	17	3	55	2	2- 8
Baker	3	1	9	0	3- 35					3- 24
					4- 36					4- 24
					5- 52					5- 48
					6- 69					6- 52
					7- 80					7- 61
					8- 97					8- 82
					9-140					9- 88
					10-144					10-100

Worcestershire won by 91 runs

Umpires : W.A.J.West and J.E.West

The scorecard from the first match at Dudley. 'Dick' Pearson scored the first first-class run at the ground when he took a single off the second over bowled by Charlie Parker and the first six was struck during Wilf Brownlee's half-century.

Sadly the pavilion at Dudley has now gone and the land is derelict. In 1985 the ground closed because of limestone mining subsidence and the club left the Birmingham League, of which they had been members since 1893. The author's father saw Walter Hammond score 265 not out for Gloucestershire there in July 1934. In the distance are the ruins of the fourteenth-century castle in the grounds of Dudley Zoo and on the superb Black Country Museum is on the same Tipton Road as the cricket ground.

The scoreboard at Dudley. Dudley was the venue for R.E. Foster's final match for Worcestershire against the 1912 Australians before his untimely death. The last time first-class cricket was played there was when Yorkshire battled out a draw, with Andrew Dalton scoring a match saving 119 not out, in July 1971.

WORCESTERSHIRE'S FIRST MATCH AT KIDDERMINSTER

Worcestershire v Glamorgan at Chester Road North, Kidderminster

9th, 11th, 12th July 1921

Toss won by Worcestershire who chose to bat.

Worcestershire	1st Innings			2nd Innings		
F.A.Pearson		b Cooper	63	c Cooper	b Nash	78
F.L.Bowley	lbw	b Nash	10		b Cooper	4
H.L.Higgins		b Bates	30		b Creber	22
*M.F.S.Jewell		b Nash	16		b Nash	14
J.W.C.Turner		b Bates	31	c Jenkins	b Nash	34
C.V.Tarbox		b Nash	13	st Jenkins	b Creber	62
C.R.Preece	c & b Nash		16	not	out	24
W.S.Gethin		b Nash	19	c Whittington	b Creber	1
W.H.Taylor	c Spiller	b Bates	8	c Clay	b Creber	11
+C.B.Ponsonby	not	out	0		b Nash	0
H.A.Gilbert	c Jenkins	b Nash	0		b Creber	0
Extras	(b 17, lb 2, w 0, nb 0)		19	(b 15, lb 6, w 1, nb 0)		22
TOTAL			225			272

Cooper	13	1	50	1	1- 25	12	1	58	1	1- 20
Nash	25	7	66	6	2- 99	29	5	76	4	2-104
Clay	9	0	32	0	3-123	7	0	25	0	3-130
Creber	6	0	18	0	4-143	25.3	3	60	5	4-133
Bates	9	1	40	3	5-170	9	1	31	0	5-211
					6-188					6-247
					7-210					7-249
					8-225					8-270
					9-225					9-271
					10-225					10-272

Glamorgan	1st Innings			2nd Innings		
*N.V.H.Riches	c Gilbert	b Taylor	28		b Pearson	4
T.A.L.Whittington	c Preece	b Taylor	34		c & b Tarbox	45
W.E.Bates	c Gethin	b Taylor	25		b Gilbert	85
E.R.Sweet-Escott	c Preece	b Taylor	0	(6) c Gethin	b Jewell	13
W.J.Spiller		b Tarbox	40	(4)	b Gilbert	23
J.C.Clay	c Preece	b Taylor	0	(5) lbw	b Jewell	15
V.L.Morris		b Taylor	5		b Tarbox	23
+W.L.T.Jenkins		b Tarbox	39	lbw	b Tarbox	9
E.Cooper		b Preece	7	c Taylor	b Gilbert	3
A.Nash		b Taylor	27		b Gilbert	1
H.Creber	not	out	0	not	out	1
Extras	(b 6, lb 7, w 0, nb 2)		15	(b 16, lb 0, w 0, nb 1)		17
TOTAL			220			239

Pearson	15	3	38	0	1- 58	13	4	36	1	1- 9
Gethin	8	0	28	0	2- 77	4	2	10	0	2- 83
Preece	4	0	19	1	3- 77	6	1	12	0	3-145
Gilbert	12	2	48	0	4-108	23.3	8	56	4	4-178
Taylor	15.2	2	64	7	5-108	9	2	53	0	5-190
Tarbox	6	2	8	2	6-126	6	0	30	3	6-205
Jewell					7-158	13	1	25	2	7-229
					8-165					8-232
					9-220					9-237
					10-220					10-239

Worcestershire won by 38 runs

Umpires : B.Brown and H.Butt

The scorecard of the first match at Kidderminster. J.W.C. Turner was the future father-in-law of Lord Runcie, the former Archbishop of Canterbury. This was the first meeting between Worcestershire and Glamorgan for twenty-three years (which had been back in Worcestershire's Minor Counties days).

The seven-acre ground was opened in 1870, but the pavilion at Kidderminster was built in 1925. There is a modern lounge bar that serves Banks's bitter and an adjoining tea room. Kidderminster played cricket here from about 1850. The present club was founded in 1890 and have been members of the Birmingham League since 1895. Don Kenyon achieved his career best innings here when he scored 259 against Yorkshire in 1956 – the highest innings against Yorkshire this century.

The old pavilion was used as a dressing room for the third eleven when two matches were being played on the arena and was brought from their previous ground in 1870 and built on its present site.

The Bournville cricket ground is on the road from Selly Oak to Kings Norton in Birmingham, so it seems strange for it to be a venue for Worcestershire cricket. In 1910, however, when Worcestershire played Essex, it was within the Worcestershire boundary. This gorgeous building was opened in June 1902. Originally a gift from the Cadbury firm (the chocolate manufacturers), it was developed by the Kent cricketing brothers George and Alec Hearne. This first match was drawn, with rain taking away the first and third days and William Burns scoring 69 out of a Worcestershire total of 108 in an hour and a quarter. The following year Surrey were the visitors for the first match of the season and Worcestershire beat a strong side that included Jack Hobbs, Tom Hayward, Ernest Hayes, Herbert Strudwick and the Aston Villa captain and English soccer international Andy Ducat. Londoner 'Dick' Pearson scored a match-winning 107 out of 301 needed to win in four hours for a two-wickets victory. Bournville has been the venue for three ICC Trophy competitions, one in 1979 and two in 1982.

Evesham has staged just one first-class match, a local derby with Gloucestershire in July 1951. Eddie Cooper scored the only century of the fixture (122), sharing a third-wicket partnership of 145 with Bob Broadbent. Gloucestershire followed-on after Reg Perks had taken 7-65 in their first innings and spinners Dick Howorth (6-67) and 'Roly' Jenkins (3-60) worked their way through the reply, leaving Worcestershire needing just 49 runs to win. They made hard work of this small target and four wickets fell before Don Kenyon hit the winning run, finishing on 33 not out. The Evesham Club was founded in the late 1800s, using this same site owned by the Rudge Estate. This photograph was taken by John Featherstone in 1984 and shows the pavilion (to the right) which was built in 1906 and the much more modern building (to the left) that is used as the tea room and bar.

Both first-class matches at Halesowen had Cambridge University as the visitors. In 1964 Mike Brearley brought a side containing Richard Hutton, Mike Griffith and Tony Windows to Seth Somers Park, but bowling by Jim Standen (7-30 in the first innings) and Basil D'Oliveira (3-20 in the second) led to a two-day, ten-wickets win after Martin Horton had scored 119. The second visit in 1969 was also over in two days with another ten-wickets win and the bowlers responsible then were Doug Slade (5-31 in the first innings) and Norman Gifford (5-54 in the second). The original wooden pavilion was gradually converted into a fine brick building and was finished in 1983. The main lounge in the pavilion is known as the Eric Hollies Lounge after the late Warwickshire and England leg-spinner, who spent the latter days of his career there.

The Hereford cricket square is set in the middle of the Westfield Racecourse and first-class cricket was first played there in 1919 when Worcestershire, who had not entered the County Championship in that first season after the First World War, met a side led by their former captain, H.K. Foster, in a two-day friendly, losing by four wickets. Immediately after this match, Foster's XI met the Australian Imperial Services side and two days later five members of Foster's side moved to New Road to play for Worcestershire against the same Australians. For the first Championship match at the ground, in 1981, Worcestershire had Glamorgan as their visitors, the game being drawn. This was followed by another draw in 1982 against Kent and the last first-class match there ended in a win for Leicestershire by five wickets. Between 1983 and 1987 three Sunday League games took place at Hereford, but Worcestershire ended their visits there when rain prevented a ball being bowled against Gloucestershire in 1988 in a Sunday League game.

In July 1980 Worcestershire made their one and only visit to Stourport-on-Severn in the County Championship, beating Lancashire by an innings. The home side batted first and scored 387 with wicketkeeper David Humphries hitting 108 not out – sharing a seventh-wicket partnership of 146 with Hartley Alleyne in 96 minutes. Alleyne scored 72, hitting 5 sixes and 6 fours. Weekend rain turned a good wicket into a sticky one and, with no play on Monday, Lancashire were bowled out twice on Tuesday with captain Nornan Gifford taking 6-14 in the first innings and 4-25 in the second.

Seven
Friends and Family

The last day of the 1990 season and the 1989 County Championship pennant is shortly to be lowered. The *Worcester Evening News* cricket correspondent, Chris Oldnall, stands underneath outside the New Road press box with Mike Beddow, of the *Daily Telegraph*, at the open window.

Don Kenyon receives a kiss on the cheek from his daughter, Susan, following the defeat of Gloucestershire at New Road to clinch the county's first Championship title in 1964, while wife, Jean, and elder daughter, Lesley, look on. On 25 April 1987, the first day of the season, Susan gave birth to Jean and Don's grandson, Daniel Kenyon Jackson. Young Daniel spent many happy hours with his grandad and is currently under the watchful eyes of Tim Curtis and Phil Newport at Worcester Royal Grammar School.

A group at Pedmore, Stourbridge in May 1971 for a Doug Slade benefit match. The players with the children are: Slade, Basil D'Oliveira (at the back), Norman Gifford and Glenn Turner (in the front). Turner is giving the author's son, Phillip (minus a few teeth), a little cuddle.

Glenn Turner broke his right ankle in a motor car accident as he was returning from one of his benefit functions towards the end of the 1978 season. At the end-of-the-season fête he is seen on the tractor signing autographs. The author's daughter, Rachel, is watching on the left of this picture. Turner returned home to Dunedin at the end of the 1982 season and in 1983 became deeply involved with the setting up and running of the Otago University and Community Sports Trust. He was appointed the New Zealand cricket manager for their 1985/86 tour of Australia, winning the three Test series 2-1. He remained coach and selector until replaced by Australian Steve Rixon in 1996.

Liam Botham in the nets at New Road during his father's time with Worcestershire. He held a twelfth birthday party in the wives' chalet at the Diglis End of New Road in August 1989, but following a Sunday League debut for Hampshire at Portsmouth against Middlesex in 1996 declined an invitation to join their staff and chose a career in rugby.

Graeme Hick caught on the way to the nets at New Road with the author's granddaughter, Catherine, perched on his 'coffin'.

Every summer there is a reunion of former Worcestershire players at New Road. They first met in 1992 when Durham were the visitors and this group attending the inaugural meeting are, from left to right: George Chesterton, Jack Flavell, Jack Birkenshaw, 'Roly, Jenkins, Grenville Wilson, Dennis Evers, Alan Spencer, Alan Brown (supported by John Inchmore), Don Kenyon, Paul Fisher, Bob Lanchbury, Alan White, Len Blunt (in front of John Aldridge), Cyril Walters (the first President of the Worcestershire Old Players Association), Norman Whiting, Geoff Darks (in front of Ted Tinkler), Tom Graveney, Dennis Summers, Rodney Cass, Brian Hall,, Duncan Fearnley (in front of Jim Yardley), Roy Barker, Alan Ormrod, 'Laddie' Outschoorn, Ted Hemsley, Henry Horton, Doug Slade, Roy Booth and Len Coldwell.

Jim Sewter's last session in the scorebox. He is pictured here with Vic Isaacs at Southampton in September 1997 as Richard Illingworth and Graeme Hick work their way through the Hampshire second innings. On the first day of this match Hick and Tom Moody had added an unbroken 438 for the third wicket – the County Championship record for that wicket – with Hick scoring 303 not out and Moody 180 not out. The match was won by Worcestershire, on the final afternoon, by nine wickets, with Hick scoring 28 not out: enough to put him at the top of the first-class batting averages. Jim Sewter began scoring for Worcestershire in the Sunday League in 1971 and was sadly missed when he died suddenly in the October following his last match.

The New Road scoreboard as Graeme Hick completes his 100th first-class hundred. This photograph was taken by Ken Edwards, a Worcestershire member. Only Wally Hammond was younger to this milestone (and only by two weeks), but Graeme is the only one to go to 100 hundreds with his second hundred scored in one match, having managed 104 in the first innings. Number two on the scoreboard was Vikram Solanki, who went on to a career best (at the time) of 155; the two batsman shared a second-wicket partnership of 243, the record for that wicket for Worcestershire against Sussex.

Graeme Hick enjoys a drink with Tom Graveney (on his left) immediately after reaching that 100th hundred. Graeme was the third batsman to complete a century of centuries while batting at New Road. Glenn Turner had hit a massive 311 not out against Warwickshire on a Saturday in May 1982 to go to his 100th and Tom Graveney had reached that magic figure with 132 against Northamptonshire in August 1964. Graeme's 100th hundred was his 73rd for Worcestershire, beating the previous record of 72 by Turner, and was followed by 119 at The Oval to complete the first four in a row for Worcestershire in first-class cricket, Graeme having hit 166 in the match at Uxbridge prior to the visit of Sussex.

Miles Illingworth, three year old son of Worcestershire's Richard, taken in 1990. Miles is now appearing in the Worcestershire under-13s and Marcus D'Oliveira has also played at this level – will either of them be the next to complete father and son appearances for Worcestershire in the future? Marcus' father, Damian, played in the same Worcestershire Second XI side as his father, Basil, against Northamptonshire at New Road in 1979. The first son to follow his father and play for Worcestershire was Herbert Isaac, who played three matches in 1919, his father, Arthur, having made 51 appearances between 1899 and 1911. Arthur was sadly killed in action at Contalmaison, France in 1916, aged forty-two – one of ten Worcestershire cricketers to lose their lives in the First World War.

David Leatherdale reading from Romans, Chapter 12, Verses 3 to 16, at the service of thanksgiving on Sunday 4 July to celebrate 100 years of first-class cricket at New Road. In the background is Lord Runcie on a return visit, nineteen years after his first:

'For I say, through the grace given unto me, to every man that is among you, not to think of himself more highly than he ought to think; but to think soberly, according as God hath dealt to every man the measure of faith. For as we have many members in one body, and all members have not the same office: So we, being many, are one body in Christ, and every one members one of another. Having then gifts differing according to the grace that is given to us, whether prophecy, let us prophesy according to the proportion of faith; Or ministry, let us wait on our ministering: or he that teacheth on teaching;

Or he is exhorteth, on exhortation: he that giveth, let him do it with simplicity; he that ruleth, with diligence; he that sheweth mercy, with cheerfulness, Let love be without dissimulation. Abhor that which is evil; in honour preferring one another; Not slothful in business; fervent in spirit; serving the Lord; Rejoicing in hope; patient in tribulation; continuing instant in prayer; Distributing to the necessity of saints; given to hospitality. Bless them which persecute you: bless and curse not. Rejoice with them that do rejoice, and weep with them that weep. Be of the same mind one toward another. Mind not high things, but condescend to men of low estate. Be not wise in your own conceits'.